"Go Watch TV!"

"Go Watch TV!"

What and how much should children really watch?

by NAT RUTSTEIN

SHEED and WARD, INC.
Subsidiary of Universal Press Syndicate
NEW YORK

This book is dedicated to the parent

CONTENTS

PREFACE

Seven-year-old Kenny has been home from school for two hours and has been sitting before the TV set ever since he dumped his books on his bed and threw his coat into the closet. He's stretched out on the living room rug, resting his head on two sofa pillows. A half of a glass of milk stands precariously on the edge of a coffee table that is arm's length away from Kenny's mouth. There are cookie crumbs on his sweater and on the rug.

Kenny's mother has finished setting the supper table and cries out, "Supper is ready." Kenny's father sits down at the table. But there is no sign of Kenny. Again, she calls Kenny. No response. A third time fails to rouse him.

"Where's Kenny?" his father asks.

"He's in the den watching TV," the mother says.

"The kid must be asleep," he suggests, and gets out of his chair to fetch his son.

When he enters the den, he notices that Kenny's eyes are wide open; the youngster is enthralled with what he's experiencing. "Didn't you hear your mother call, son?" he asks.

"What?" Kenny asks.

The exasperated father repeats what he said the first time—but in a louder, harsher voice.

All Kenny can say is, "Wait, I want to see this," without ever taking his eyes off the TV tube.

Infuriated, the father storms over to the TV set, turns it off, yanks Kenny off the floor, shoves the youngster out of the den and yells, "Go into the kitchen and eat your supper."

"Go Watch TV!" is meant to help parents deal with situations like this and with other common sticky situations related to children's television watching at home. With both television and children in the home every day, parents sometimes wonder whether there's any harm in gazing at the tube, but most of the time they forget about the interplay between the two. In fact, many parents frankly or secretly are delighted to have a TV set in the home so they can use it as a baby-sitter.

Well, TV can be harmful. Television is a mighty force, and even many people who work in the industry aren't aware of its power to shape attitudes, beliefs, and even personalities. Their ignorance of the capacity of TV to influence behavior and values is almost as serious as that of a radiologist who doesn't know the power potential of the instrument he works with.

A major purpose of this book is to make parents appreciate what kind of force their children are interacting with when they turn on the TV set and what the consequences can be if parents make no attempt to control TV watching in the home.

Actually, *"Go Watch TV!"* rings an alarm—a sounding, I feel, that is desperately needed. Vested interest groups have tried to cloud the dangers associated with televiewing. This book tries to dispel those clouds, dealing with the reality of television as a medium many people worship. It illustrates what effect TV can have on children. It points out the damage it has wrought in the past twenty-five years. But on the other hand, it recognizes TV's power for good and demonstrates how it can be used as a positive social force. Some books and articles have been written about television and its impact on people, especially children, but much of the literature has escaped the grasp of the parent.

The little that has been produced in academic circles is flavored with professional language, making it difficult for the average parent to understand. And, the material put together for the lay community has painted a rather fuzzy picture of the effect TV has on children, leaving parents confused—a state in which, perhaps, some vested interest groups would like the parent to remain. On the other hand, there have been attempts by writers to treat the subject objectively, presenting the evidence on both sides of the controversy, and thus putting the parent in a position of making a judgment: Should they do something about controlling TV watching in their home? What usually happens is that the concerned parent weighs both sides, finds both arguments fairly persuasive, can't turn to anyone to help him evaluate each side's case, and finally gives up, making no changes in the TV-watching pattern of his children, which in most homes is complete freedom to watch what they please and for as long as they wish.

But the average parent isn't the only one who is confused by some of the literature and studies that have been produced. Distinguished newspapers and magazines which have to make judgments and reveal them to the public have misinterpreted findings related to TV's impact on children. The reporting of the results of the U.S. Surgeon General's report on the effect of televised vio-

lence on children is a case in point. Many newspapers ran
stories stating that violence on television doesn't affect
the behavior of children. Only a protest by many of the
scientists who worked on the study forced some of the
papers to run retractions. The scientists felt that their
work demonstrated that TV *does*, indeed, affect children's behavior.

The impact of television on children is a complicated
problem. Most psychologists and neurologists agree that
what humans perceive is stored in their brains perma-
nently. They even go on to say that one's early perceptions and experiences as a child actually influence the
very structure of his brain. Certainly when kids watch TV
they perceive quite a bit. We know also that what people
perceive and experience contributes to the development
of a person's behavior. All of this is difficult to measure.

The crucial point is: should parents wait for conclusive
proof of TV's impact on children's behavior before putting the brakes on permissive TV watching, before developing a sensible TV-viewing plan in their home?

Some people would argue that it would be unfair to the
TV industry or, for that matter, to the children, to take
drastic action without a thorough scientific investigation
of TV's effect on kids. The trouble with that argument—and I'm afraid that argument has held sway for
much too long—is that studying the effect of television on
children's behavior is a lot more crucial than studying the
effect Tiddly Winks has on the human thumb.

Besides, if there is considerable evidence that TV
shapes human attitudes, values, and personality, should
parents allow their children to continue to pursue their
televiewing habits until conclusive proof of adverse effects is revealed? The best way to answer that question is

to raise another question: Would it be fair to children to gamble with their emotional and physical health in order to be fair in the controversy over TV's influence on behavior? After all, it might take a lifetime before scientists unearth conclusive proof.

A lot has happened in the twenty-five years since television became a popular medium in the United States. And much of what has happened—the good and the bad—was influenced and, at times, even fashioned directly by television. *"Go Watch TV!"* explains how.

This book is not a traditional piece of scholarship. It is a point of view that is supported by evidence. And it is purposely put together in this form to give parents a clearer picture of a problem that has been sorely neglected for much too long—a problem, I deeply feel, that has seriously affected the young people of our country.

My hope is that *Go Watch TV!"* will do more than alert parents to television's capacity to harm or strengthen human development. I have tried to show parents how to help their children overcome their dependency on TV while not damning television, how to gain control of the medium instead of allowing it to control them and their children.

While I have spent three years researching this book, I have also drawn heavily on my fifteen years of experience in commercial television, my present profession as an educator, and my experience as a father of four children. Aware of my lack of expertise in psychology, I have worked closely with several people in the Psychology Department of the University of Massachusetts, benefiting from their professional guidance. I have had ample opportunity to see what impact TV has had on its viewers, especially children. What I have observed has frightened me and led me to write this book.

I do not view the television industry as an enemy. In fact, my hope is that the people working in TV, representing all strata of that profession, will cooperate in creating programs that will not damage children, but rather will aid their development as healthy human beings.

My most ardent wish is that the parents who read this book will be inspired to control the use of television in their homes and find the time and energy to carry out their intentions.

1

A Real "Live" Teacher

A mother's hands are in the kitchen sink, deep in soap suds; her eye catches the oven clock. "Oops, the cake will be ready in four minutes," she mutters to herself. When she remembers that the baby should be awake soon, her two older children start arguing over who got to the club chair first. Desperate, the young mother cries out to the battling boys, "Go watch TV." The boys run to the television set and the dispute ends as soon as the TV is clicked on.

"Peace!" the mother exclaims. "Peace." Many parents, college educated and noneducated, black and white, poor and rich, use television as an electronic pacifier. It is a convenient, effective means, they feel, of preventing children from getting into mischief. Some parents who want a low noise level in the home use TV to anesthetize their children when they are indoors. Other mothers and fathers who feel they don't have the time to talk to their children or play with them use television as a baby-sitter.

As a modern American parent who is assailed by mounting family and community responsibilities and social pressure and who cherishes a few moments of quiet at home from time to time, I know how tempting it is to employ TV as an electronic pacifier, anesthetizer, or baby-sitter. I have used it in all three ways, securing the intended results.

But three years ago I became aware of the need to stop that practice after noticing what effect the electronic pacifier was having on my daughter, then two and a half years old.

One day Valerie came to me after dinner, looked me straight in the eye, threw out her little chubby arms, bumped like a stripper, and belted out that famous cigarette commercial: "You can take Salem out of the country, but, you can't take the country out of Salem." Valerie completed her flawless performance by taking a drag on an imaginary cigarette. Struck speechless, I hunched over and looked at my daughter as I had never looked at her before. This baby, still in diapers, I thought, was being reached and taught by TV; but I shuddered at the thought that followed: What else is TV teaching her?

Like so many other people, I had considered television a harmless instrument of pleasure. For twenty years I believed that myth, never giving any thought to how it was affecting people, especially children.

Valerie's performance was not unique. Many children around her age express what they learn on television.

One thing seems certain, most preschoolers who watch TV are reached and taught by it. For example, psychologists Jack Lyle and Heidi R. Hoffman found in a study done for the U.S. Surgeon General's Office that 76 percent of the three-year-olds they tested could name their favorite program and 87 percent of the children could identify the cartoon character Fred Flintstone.[1]

In another Lyle and Hoffman study, 75 percent of the three hundred mothers of first graders they interviewed reported that their youngsters sing jingles they learned from television.[2] TV is even affecting children younger than two. Dr. Dan Anderson, a child psychologist at the University of Massachusetts, reports that one parent he had been seeing told him her eight-month-old child, who watched color TV for about six hours a day, would cry if the set was turned off.[3]

Television is a powerful teacher—and dangerous because we are not aware of being taught when watching it. Information and knowledge seem to seep into our consciousness without our knowing it. Values are inculcated and we become acculturated.

We have been conditioned to think that learning has to be a bore, taking place in a sterile classroom with a stern-faced middle-aged spinster standing over us, empowered to drum "knowledge" into our heads. Television teaches, painlessly, wounding us without our knowing it, but also enriching us, expanding our outlook on life, without our knowing it.

Television teaches how to throw an uppercut, seduce the opposite sex, hurl a hand grenade. Turn on a detective series, a soap opera, or a war movie and you will see what I mean. The fact is that kids learn behavior simply by watching others.[4] When you seriously consider how much children watch others on TV, you know their behavior development has to be influenced by their experiences with television. Observant parents have noticed their children gesturing and posturing like their TV heroes and heroines, even adopting some of their verbal expressions and speech patterns. Yes, kids are learning from the programs and commercials they watch, even from shows like *Love American Style, Hawaii Five O,* and *Mannix.*

However, what they learn should concern their parents. As Harvard psychologist Dr. Gerald Lesser puts it: "If you show [a child] that people relate with violence, that's what he'll learn; if people treat each other with respect, that's what he'll learn."[5]

Television can also expand a child's knowledge in positive ways. My daughter, who three years ago was running around singing cigarette jingles, now knows all of the letters in the alphabet, can count and make some sense of numbers, and enjoys identifying triangles, squares, circles, and rectangles in inanimate and live objects. *Sesame Street* has made that possible. *Mister Rogers* is educating her also, teaching her to be thoughtful and to respect others, teaching her that "sugar dissolves in water but sand does not." *Captain Kangaroo* is teaching her to appreciate beauty and other cultures, to love animals and to pop corn.

Valerie and her friends and millions of other children are learning about life in their country and other countries by watching television. Every day that they watch TV, they learn something new. Charles Silberman, the author of *Crisis in the Classroom,* thinks "students probably learn more about certain subjects from television than from [their] schools."[6] Marshall McLuhan, a modern prophet of electronic communications, feels that by the time a child enters school, he has already had five years of adult education—thanks to TV.[7] My twelve-year-old son learned more about our judicial process by watching Perry Mason than by attending social studies classes. Because of televising of space ship journeys to the moon, kids today know more about astronomy, rocketry, and geology than the kids in the 1940s and 1950s did. They are more socially aware. They also know that racism exists in our country, for they have seen the themes of racial prejudice and intermarriage on popular programs like *Bonanza.* They have seen riots, disputes, and demonstrations on newscasts. But they have also learned antisocial behavior—how to shoot a machine gun, rob a bank, eliminate a sentry quietly, and kick an enemy in the groin—from programs like *Cannon, Mission: Impossible, Gunsmoke,* and *It Takes a Thief.*

Television teaches well. It plays a major role in fashioning the shape and soul of our society. To deny that it does is to pull down the window shade and proclaim there is no sun.

What is it about TV that makes it an effective teacher? There are several factors. Television is able to capture a child's attention, arouse his curiosity. To teach someone, you must be able to reach him first, and TV is a master at reaching.

TV is able to reach kids, because kids believe TV never punishes. It provides youngsters with pleasure, thrills them, shows them things, places, and people they have never seen before. It keeps them from being lonely; it cheers them up when they are sad; it shows them affection when none is forthcoming from anyone else in their home. It is a trusted friend, because it rarely fails to reward them.

Kids also like TV because it provides them with a sense of power. By simply turning the dial they can switch scenes, changing moods and images. They are in control, calling the shots, a situation they rarely experience outside of the TV-viewing room, for there's always Mom and Dad telling them what they can or cannot do, and in school the teacher seems to be always issuing instructions. When left alone with TV, kids are the boss.

So for television—a teacher kids don't consider a teacher—the child is a rapt and willing student.

But there is a deeper reason why TV teaches well. Television excels in drawing people to itself, especially kids, even casting a spell over them. It is not unusual to see children rise early, turn on the set, plunk down before it, and just stare at a test pattern.

Television is an involving medium. "It makes man participate," says Marshall McLuhan, "and become involved with his whole being . . . ."[8] Most children demonstrate that behavior every time they watch TV. Their involvement is evidenced by their desire to move closer to the set, by their desire to join their TV friends in chasing bandits or trying to assemble the letter W. There is a deep urge to crawl into the set, to become one with the source of their pleasure. However, though they love their TV friends, their gravitation toward the set is motivated by a greater love—their love for the fascinating force of television itself.

If you have ever observed kids watching television you would know what I mean. Put them ten feet away from a set and by the end of the program they will have slipped out of their seat and inched—often unconsciously—closer to the tube. They are being drawn by television, being enticed by it, wanting to embrace the fascinating cool light that is being beamed at them. In experiencing television, McLuhan states, the viewer is the screen.[9] The set only acts as a funnel for the TV signal or message that may originate thousands of miles away.

Then if McLuhan is right (and I feel he is) what happens to the real TV screen—the human being when he turns on the set and becomes involved with the television experience? After all, a human screen is a lot different from the textile fabric screens films are projected on. We are not made of nylon. We are sensitive creatures composed of nerves, bones, muscle, blood, a mind and spirit.

Hopefully, one day the psychological and medical communities will discover exactly what television does to its "screens."

Some teachers have noticed kids' involvement with

**Pictures a kindergarten student drew of himself watching television
for teacher Marilyn Marchand**

television taking place while they experience TV. Marilyn Marchand of the Ware, Massachusetts, public school system had an eye-opening experience with one of her kindergarten students. She had the boy, who was five and one-half years old, draw himself watching television. The three pictures he drew are on page 7.

After the drawing session, which only lasted a few minutes, the boy explained his sketches to Ms. Marchand. She recorded the conversation and shared with me his interpretation of his drawings and her own feelings about the boy's effort:

"The first two pictures he called, 'Me Watching Cartoons.' There is a happy smiling face inside the set. This is Billy's face. The third picture is entitled 'Me and Big Bird.' The square shape of the television has disappeared. In its place are two circles, one on top of the other. The top circle is a face—the same smiling face that appears in the other pictures. On the sides of the lower circle are the dials and the speaker. I pointed to the face and asked, 'Who is this?' 'That's me,' Billy said. 'And where is Big Bird?' I asked. Billy then pointed to the face again. 'You and Big Bird are the same?' 'Yes,' he replied. Billy, Big Bird, and the television had become one and the same."

Child psychologist Dr. Dan Anderson had a similar experience. He had a four-year-old boy draw himself watching *Mister Rogers Neighborhood.* The youngster produced five drawings in about thirty minutes. The sketches show the child surrendering himself, little by little, to television. In the first drawing, the boy appears bigger than the television set; in the second drawing, the set remains about the same size with more detail in the screen, but the boy shrinks in size; in the next one the set becomes larger, so does the screen and he not only is smaller but his arms are missing; in the fourth picture

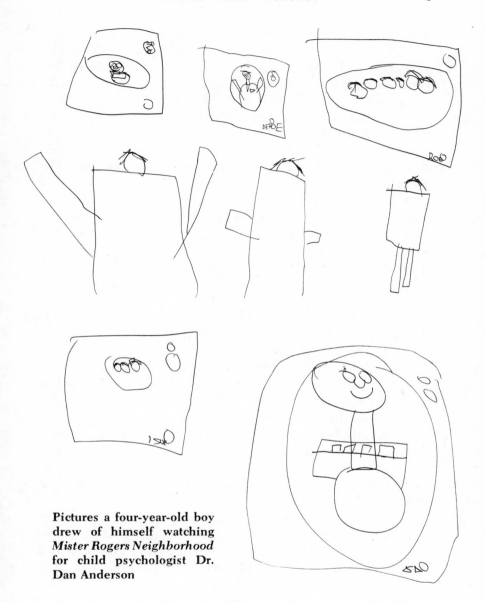

Pictures a four-year-old boy drew of himself watching *Mister Rogers Neighborhood* for child psychologist Dr. Dan Anderson

there is no sign of the boy, only the big TV set. In a sense, the boy's secret wish had been fulfilled; he vicariously was able to play with his TV friends inside the set. In the last picture, we see a huge TV set with a big happy-looking figure inside the set. That, the boy told his mother, was Mr. Rogers saying goodbye. Where is the boy in the picture? I suspect he is with his TV friends—inside the set. Obviously, that mental and emotional excursion into the land of *Mister Rogers Neighborhood* is temporary. How long that flight lasted was not measured.

About four months later, Dr. Anderson had that same four-year-old boy do the same exercise. This time the boy drew himself watching *The Wild, Wild West* show. His output was smaller, but his renderings conveyed the same message as his initial effort: He became so involved with television that he surrendered himself to it, becoming the TV experience.

In the first drawing, the boy is bigger than the TV set. In the second one, the set is bigger and the boy has shrunk. On the tube is a cowboy who has just killed his enemy. The cowboy appears satisfied with his achievement. In the last drawing, there is no TV set, just a big picture of a happy cowboy with his arms raised, as if he were signaling to whoever could see that he had just triumphed. There is no TV set in this drawing, I feel, because the boy and the cowboy had fused, become one. When the child drew the last picture, the cowboy and his surroundings were so real to him that mentally he left his home surroundings.

Television can be hypnotic according to Dr. Harry Goodall, who teaches hypnosis to medical students at the University of Alabama: "Television programmers and advertisers have the TV viewer when he is relaxed, his conscious mind distracted, his emotions aroused, and they can implant repeated messages in his mind, many

Pictures drawn four months later for Dr. Dan Anderson by the same child of himself watching _The Wild, Wild West_ show

on a subconscious level. These are all conditions necessary for an effective hypnotic session. Once hypnotized
by TV, people are influenced to a degree they would
hardly believe possible."[10]

Television is more than involving and hypnotic. For
some people TV involvement leads to addiction. Psychiatrist Joost Meerlo recognized TV's addictive quality
back in 1954, when he wrote in the *Journal of Nervous
and Mental Disease:* "Television fascination is a real
addiction, that is to say, television can become a habit-
forming device, the influence of which cannot be
stopped without active therapeutic interference. . . . As in all mass media, we have to be aware of
the hypnotizing, seductive action of this all penetrating
form of communication. People become fascinated even
when they do not want to look on."[11]

Psychoanalyst Donald Kaplan describes how TV addiction affects a human being: "His watching overrides
his intention to perform even ordinary actions such as
answering mail and returning phone calls. It soon overrides his intention to go to sleep at a particular hour.
There is no internal motive strong enough to interrupt
the behavior. Only external circumstances may interrupt
it—a standing appointment, an incoming phone call, etc.
Otherwise the behavior terminates in sleep."[12]

A West German study reported by *Time* magazine
revealed that TV addicts experience psychological with-
drawal symptoms, including moodiness, child spanking,
wife beating, extramarital affairs and, at home, decreased
interest in sex along with few orgasms. The article noted:
"The society asked 184 habitual viewers to renounce the
tube for a year. At first they seemed happy to be free of it.
They went to the movies three times as often, and spent
twice as much time reading and playing games. Before
long, however, they felt a renewed urge to watch TV.

Though the subjects were paid for every day of self denial, one man resumed his habit after only three weeks. No one held out for more than five months.

"What drove them back to the tube was mounting tension at work, at home and in bed. Quarreling and physical aggression increased. Before the sets were switched off, only 2% of the husbands had ever beaten their wives and only 58% of the parents had disciplined their children by slapping them. Afterward, however, the percentages rose to 5 and 66. With TV on again, aggression decreased and sexual habits went back to normal—except for a while, husbands and wives had a few more orgasms than they were used to and single people masturbated more than ever before."[13]

University of Michigan psychiatrist Derek Miller sees some correlation between a youth's drug taking and his TV watching as a child: "There is a remarkable similarity between those adolescents who take drugs for their vivid visual impressions, which they inertly and passively sit and watch within picture frames of their own minds, and those who sit as small children in equivalent positions watching a television screen"[14]

After exploring the research of scientists Jean Houston and Robert Masters on altered states of consciousness, *New York Times* religious editor Edward Fiske suggests that "people watching television for long periods of time may actually go into states of trance and become hyper-suggestible." He adds: "This is something that cries for serious research."[15]

2

The Good and Bad
of Television

Television has no conscience, intelligence, or emotions, nor is it a respecter of persons. It is completely subservient to its creator, man. Whatever it teaches is the result of human creativity and effort, reflecting man's condition. This is apparent even in TV's fictional episodes like those of *Bonanza*. Most of them are based on our most pressing social, economic, political, and spiritual problems: drugs, poverty, political corruption, war, the struggle for self-awareness. Even shows based in celestial settings like *Star Trek* deal with contemporary earthly emotional and psychological conflicts with which most viewers can identify: the drive for recognition, status, power; temptations to cheat, lie; the soul struggle between selfishness and selflessness; love and hate.

Since man is the fashioner of television, the greatest of all mass communications media, he can shape it into a monster, or program it to be a catalyst for social good and intellectual enlightenment. Man has done both, leaving television like man, somewhat schizophrenic.

Television has helped to unite the world physically. By way of a camera aboard a rocketship roaring to the

14

moon, we have seen our beautiful blue and white planet, round and one. We have watched a human step out of his spacecraft onto the dust of the moon. Through a communications satellite, television covers a news story halfway around the world and beams it live into millions of homes in almost every land. Television has awakened our social consciousness: we have seen vicious police dogs attack black children, the burning of black churches, Dr. Martin Luther King crying out to nearly two hundred thousand people at the Freedom March in Washington, "I have a dream, Lord," Dr. King's assassination, his funeral. All of this and more on network television helped white America begin to feel what black America has felt for three hundred years. The woman's rights struggle, youth's cry for help, for independence, for a more compassionate world—that too has been vividly communicated to the consciousness of Americans. The abuse and injustice heaped upon the American Indian have also been drummed home.

Television has exposed war as it really is—an ugly, sickening, terrifying human act, dashing forever—hopefully—the exalted station of the warrior. The pain and agony of Vietnam and Cambodia have been felt by millions of people outside those tortured lands. They have seen blood spilled, life snuffed out, homes set afire, refugees running from the reach of death, bombs blasting villages, young men fighting for a cause they don't understand, naked and dazed babies crying beside the bodies of their dead parents. Through television they have seen every aspect of war and they have been inspired to cry out for peace in a way never before witnessed; they have literally shaken the gates of government, forcing a heartsick president not to seek a second term.

In a way, television has changed childhood as generations before experienced it. Today's children are beginning to count, read, and write at three because of programs like *Sesame Street*. They have been exposed to more places, more things, more concepts than the child of yesteryear. Children are taken on animal explorations all over the world through the program *Wild Kingdom;* Walt Disney productions show them how families in different lands live; *Zoom* inspires them to make films, sing, and dance.

Watching national political party conventions not only sharpens a child's political awareness, but also helps adults overcome certain myths about the American political processes that were established and perpetuated by pre-TV elementary and secondary schools. Watching how the local city council and town board function also helps develop a more knowledgeable, wiser electorate. We have seen the results of all of this on TV: More citizens, young and old, the previously disenfranchised, even some former cynics, demanding—sometimes with deep poignancy—change in traditional political practices, in the development of governmental policies and party selection of candidates. Television has been a significant factor in penetrating political puffery and party propaganda and exposing to the American public how the American system really operates. That kind of penetration has been accompanied by protest and pain on the part of those who wish to preserve the status quo. And that too has been seen on TV.

Television has helped Americans become more honest about their country. It has exposed its imperfections as well as perfections, helping to disprove America's infallibility to its inhabitants and to people in other lands. It has framed and put into focus the problems that plague our society: ecological plundering, racism, the family-unit breakdown, sexism, the labor and corporate conflict, the search for identity and purpose in life.

The fact that there is much that has to be done to improve our way of life became more apparent to all of us when we watched for hours the funerals of John F. Kennedy, Dr. Martin Luther King, Jr., and Robert Kennedy.

Television has helped to expose the "American Dream" as a delusion and prompted the courageous to begin forging a new national vision based on society's real potential.

Television is helping human beings to overcome cultural barriers and provincialism, exposing the customs, religions, and traditions of people everywhere. Through it, strangeness, which was once mocked, is now being respected, and attempts are being made to understand it. For example, black and white people more than ever before understand the meaning and value of the American Indian stomp dance. They have learned to respect it. The family living on a South Dakota prairie farm today has a better understanding of the farm family in the Soviet Ukraine than they might have had twenty-five years ago. Some TV documentaries have shown Americans that Africa is not a continent ruled by Tarzan, but that it is a vast stretch of land with a varied topography, different climates, a large variety of cultures and subcultures, and black, brown, and white people whose heritage roots spring from once proud and ancient civilizations. In many respects, television has broadened our vision, making us more world conscious and more and more aware of the reality of the oneness of mankind.

But television can hurt human beings too, physically as well as emotionally. It can teach and reinforce antisocial behavior. There is evidence that exposure to cops and robbers, cowboy and Indian "shoot 'em ups," the eye-gouging, head-knocking antics of the *Three Stooges*, the *Roadrunner*, and *Popeye*—those programs and ones like them—can stimulate aggressive behavior in children. On the other hand, a daily dose of the blood spilling in Southeast Asia on the evening news has made some people, including some kids, indifferent toward human suffering, pain, even death. In a way, that can be as socially damaging as being stimulated by TV to punch someone in the face.

The day-after-day exposure to the storm of commercials has developed in many children a lust for things; they have turned into budding materialists. This form of media brainwashing has affected the child-parent relationship. Persuaded by TV to get a toy, a child pressures his parents to buy him the advertised article, never concerned about the money involved or the intrinsic worth of the item. Parents—against their better judgment—usually give in to maintain domestic tranquility. A vicious cycle is started: Child watches commercial; child badgers parent to purchase advertised item; parent bows to the child's wish which usually is more like a demand. And the cycle seems never ending. The price the parent pays is more than the cost of the toy or box of cereal. For one thing, the parents begin to hate themselves for doing something their intuition tells them is wrong, and for another, the child seems locked into a process of poor value development. These two factors then become part of the basis of a communications gap between child and parent. Cornell University psychologist Dr. John Condry has noticed this pattern. This is what he told the Federal Trade Commission on November 10, 1971: "I believe advertisements directed toward children may seriously interfere with family life by creating conflicts between parents and children, by teaching children to be materialistic, and by disrupting attempts to teach the child responsibility."[1]

Through TV many people see places and living situations that they would never be able to experience. While this could be illuminating, it could also set off social frustration in children. Consider a child living in a flat in a poor urban neighborhood, paint peeling off the walls, roaches trooping across a bare, splintered floor, the only window facing a soot-coated brick wall, watching a program like *My Three Sons* or *Leave It to Beaver.* He must wonder why he doesn't have his own room, a yard to play in, a fireplace in the living room, a brand new shiny car, and parents who are immaculately dressed, always calm and smiling. Too many poor city kids learn to hate the society that gives to some the luxury they see on TV and to them the living misery in their midst. And some learn to hate their parents, preferring the idealized parents on television. But middle-class kids are not immune to this kind of social frustration. They, too, see a kind of life style on TV family shows which they admire and which doesn't exist in their homes. Many of them have wandered off to New York's Greenwich Village, to San Francisco's Haight-Ashbury, to hundreds of communes throughout the United States, and to drug-culture communities abroad seeking something they couldn't find at home—something that was promised them on TV.

There's racism on television. And tragically, those who shape the programs, who act in them, for the most part, are unaware of their racist thinking, their racist actions. It is not the kind of damage that a bomb creates; it quietly tears away the pride of those viewers whose race, religion, or nationality is belittled; it bolsters the warped notions that many people have of certain ethnic groups. Imagine what runs through an American Indian child's mind when he sees Indians on TV portrayed as savages. And what the white middle-class preschooler is learning about the original inhabitants of our land when he sees the same program.

Children are being introduced to sex through television. Soap operas, variety shows like *Laugh-In*, detective series and commercials use sex to draw viewer attention to their programs or messages. Many of those viewers, unfortunately, are three, four, five, six, seven, and eight-year-olds. Kathy McMeel, a Detroit news journalist, described the kind of sex-oriented fare most young children are exposed to when watching TV in an article she wrote for her newspaper:

"A love goddess runs down the beach, waves nibbling at her toes, her blond streaked hair sweeping back behind wide, expectant eyes. A flimsy garment clings to every supple curve. She runs faster, arms open, until finally she throws herself breathlessly into HIS arms. . . .

"Where is this scene? Right in your living room, that's where.

"Wild and passionately aroused, she can't stop herself. She runs her fingers through his hair, knocks his glasses off and kisses him again. . . .

"What's watching? Your nine-year-old daughter as she sits on her stuffed panda bear and wipes jelly off her face.

"Now a smoldering tigress herself lies on a tiger-skin rug, teasing, beckoning. Through wet sensuous lips she purrs a dare: Are you man enough for her?

"Is who man enough for her? Your goggly-eyed male offspring, twelve, who's waiting for 'Land of the Giants' or 'Gunsmoke' to come back on and who has only just begun to have faint notions of what this boy-girl stuff's all about. . . ."[2]

Too many American kids spend more time watching TV than any other activity. This condition could be damaging to a child's emotional and physical well-being. By spending most of their time gazing at the tube, children miss the experience of playing with other children.

This is a necessary experience, because it is here that a child learns to relate to his peer group, starts learning how to negotiate in the world outside of his home—a facility necessary in the development of a strong, well-rounded adult. Too much TV watching can also rob a child of the experience of mastering the operation of certain basic tools, thus impeding the development of his motor skills. And there is another danger: The child may learn to be a watcher and not a doer—a spectator and not a participant.[3]

Turning on a TV set causes no pain; nor does watching it. Yet there is a possibility that televiewing could be physically harmful. X-ray emission from television sets could be injurious to human beings. Watching too much TV too close to a set might be damaging to a viewer's eyes. How many parents who monitor the way their children watch television are aware of how close their kids are to the set or whether they watch with or without a light?

Much more could be written about the positive and negative aspects of television. The point is that television is here, ever present and impartial as to who it is helping and hurting. Television has taken root in America. Ninety-seven percent of American homes have at least one TV set. There are more TV sets in homes than indoor toilets and telephones. In most towns the TV antenna is as commonplace as the chimney. *TV Guide* has the largest circulation of any magazine in America. Television is here, all of it—the good and bad—captivating minds, capturing people's time, gaining in popularity.

According to the Neilsen Television Index, "Overall household usage increased substantially this past season. The weekly average of 43 hours and 24 minutes per TV household was one hour and 10 minutes above year-ago levels."[4]

Some angry critics of television view this movement as

a dangerous encroachment on the American way of
life—a movement which could sap our people's vitality,
turning them into lethargic, apathetic citizens, slaves to a
force they have no direct way of shaping, no way of
influencing. Their means of blocking TV's seizure of the
American soul is severe: Eliminate TV! Such drastic
action would be like eliminating the automobile because
there are too many of them. But the extremists among TV
critics are not pointing to an imaginary monster in media.
There are aspects of television that are monstrous, and
the fact that television's popularity is growing without
much improvement in the quality of programming, without much sensitivity toward the damage that programs
can have on audiences—that is, indeed, frightening. But
the thought of eliminating television is equally frightening. On the other hand, something has to be done. To do
nothing would be tantamount to sanctioning the contin-
uation of the video pollution that seeps into the minds of
millions of children and adults every day.

Doing nothing is as risky as a motorist's ignoring a
traffic light on a heavily traveled intersection. What is the
answer? Certainly not ignoring the problem or eliminating TV. Yet an answer is needed. Even people connected
with the TV industry recognize the need for a change in
the direction television has taken. It is needed, producer
Eliot A. Daley feels, for the sake of our children:
"Through television, our children's lives are inundated
with death and disaster one moment, trivia and banality
the next, cemented together with the sixty second mortar
of manipulation and materialism. Their experience is
very different from ours. In the matter of violence alone,
their formative years are bathed in blood of which we
only recently have taken notice."[5]

While deeply concerned people—people of all walks
of life—express anxiety over what television is doing to

children, there are others, especially television network spokesmen, who respond in a polite, often patronizing manner, claiming no one has proven conclusively that TV hurts children. They are right! But then no one has proven conclusively that smoking cigarettes causes lung cancer. Yet the United States Surgeon General, based on heaps of evidence, launched a vigorous campaign against cigarette smoking. Finally, Congress ordered cigarette advertising banned on TV and radio. He began an anti-smoking campaign on the broadcasting media. Cigarette companies were forced to print health warnings on all of their packs and newspaper and magazine ads.

But it is easier to take action against cigarette smoking because its apparent effects on people are more visible than those of television. We have seen and heard the smoker's cough; nonsmokers are continually exposed to cigarette smoke and ashes; and we've viewed films of the difference between a nonsmoker's lungs and a smoker's lungs. Television, on the other hand, doesn't blow smoke in your face or drop ashes on your hair. In fact, it brings most of us pleasure and takes us to places and people we have dreamt and read about, but have never seen. Naturally, you don't find fault or seriously question something that gives you so much fun, that does not ridicule you, laugh at you, backbite, or punch you in the mouth. For most of us, it is an experience we rarely find in the street, in the marketplace, or in another person's home. TV comforts us, never punishes us—only rewards. *Television Quarterly* observed, "Watching TV is like making love—not a reasoning activity. The very addictive quality hooks us. . . ."[6]

Americans' general satisfaction with existing television fare is not the only reason why there has been no concerted effort to find out how television affects children. For years the television industry has been busy building a favorable image of itself. If it can sell soap, it can certainly sell itself! Often angry complaints by concerned parents have been brushed aside very smoothly by industry spokesmen as meaningless, emotional outbursts by powerless people. The National Association of Broadcasters, the voice of the industry, maintains a propaganda center called the Television Information Office. It is supported financially by the three commercial networks and more than one hundred TV stations. They not only send out propaganda to "4,500,000 influential" people and institutions regularly, they have produced more than forty publications which defend commercials and argue against changing the existing TV structure. They also engage in research, measuring viewers' likes and dislikes of television programming. Their findings are usually self-serving and end up in news releases which they prepare and distribute to the news media across the land.

Some of these efforts are absurd. One was done by Bruskin Associates which showed that the public does not believe television to be an important cause of violent behavior.[7] These findings were revealed to the public as if their researchers had made a significant breakthrough in settling the raging controversy concerning the effect of televised violence on children. With all due respect for the public, it is not equipped to make a professional judgment on such a sensitive scientific matter. If twelve years ago the average person on the street had been polled about the possibility of humans walking on the moon in ten years he would have rejected the idea as an hallucination.

Hundreds of thousands of dollars are spent yearly by the industry to maintain the Television Information Office. But it appears they will be spending more money in the near future, for the consensus at the National Association of Broadcasters' 1972 convention was that there was an urgent need to improve television's image across the land. After all, a convincing "good guy" image is an effective way of keeping the public satisfied with the TV fare, thus preventing any public outcry for serious investigations of TV's effect on kids. The industry czars know that only a grass-roots rebellion against the present TV establishment could crack their hold on the medium. So they will do almost anything to keep the public in its present stupor, believing that commercial television is doing a great job.

It is tragic that so much time was devoted to talking about the industry's image at the NAB convention and that so little was mentioned about cleaning up and improving the quality of children's TV programs and commercials.

The industry's efforts to protect its "good guy" image are not always confined to elaborate, expensive advertising and public relations campaigns. Survival energy is expended in quiet conference rooms or offices in Washington, D.C. The National Association of Broadcasters operates from a $2.6 million office building in the nation's capital with a large staff. These people lobby vigorously to block broadcasting reform. In fact, they were instrumental in getting Congress to thwart the Federal Communications Commission's effort to limit the number of commercials.[8]

When the federal government decides to explore some aspect of commercial television, the industry's reflex is quick and powerful. The U.S. Surgeon General's investigation on the effects of televised violence on children is a case in point.[9] ABC and NBC, for example, were able to keep seven outstanding scientists off the investigatory team. Some of these people had already published studies indicating a strong causal relationship between TV violence and adolescent aggression. Some of the slots were given to scientists with close ties to the industry.[10]

Those representing the networks were dogged in keeping the investigation from besmirching the image of television. Their attempt to water down, to soften the scientists' findings was successful. It was so successful that the public is still baffled as to what the U.S. Surgeon General's investigation actually discovered. That kind of fuzzy result must have set off some chuckles in the executive suites of the three networks.

What is sad is that many of the people who run our TV stations and networks are, for the most part, decent human beings; many have families and only want the best for their children. The trouble is they have lost perspective on the meaning of life. They have buried themselves in their work and with each passing year have become more deeply involved—in fact, so involved that it is easy for them to rationalize their industry's efforts in children's programming as good for children. Besides, most people want to believe that what they are doing professionally is not hurting anyone. And the people who call the shots in TV are no exception.

One frequently expressed rationalization they use for their Saturday morning storm of cartoons and late afternoon reruns is that children, like adults, need some relief from the rigors of their job. Going to school, they point out, is like going to work. So they provide them with episodes in which they can escape. There is trouble with that kind of thinking. To put it bluntly, it is inconsistent. It presupposes that TV does not teach, that the violence, sex, racism, and materialism that emerge from the TV set won't affect the children who are watching. Yet these same people are busy trying to solicit advertisers to use TV to teach children about the virtues of their products.

Is it that program content does *not* teach and commercials do?

Commercial television has been serving the American people for more than twenty-five years with very little interference from either the government or the public in the way of programming and advertising restrictions. The industry has enjoyed the privilege of policing its own affairs with some distant assistance from the Federal Communications Commission. The Surgeon General's ban on cigarette ads was probably the sternest governmental action taken against the TV industry. But that came about only after a costly, agonizing controversy that dragged on for years.

Commercial television appeared in the United States in the late 1940s. Its popularity soared. In 1950, 9 percent of the American homes had TV sets; today nearly every home has a set and 39 percent of the households have two or more sets.[11] For most people TV is their primary source of information and culture. Most people turn on television for the news; the average American child spends almost twice as much time watching TV as sitting in a classroom; and according to the Neilsen Television Index children between the ages of three and five spent approximately 64 percent of their waking hours watching television.[12]

Today television is so powerful an influence on Americans that in most homes it has been adopted as a member of the family. For the lonely, it is a companion. Many elderly people, practically forgotten by their children, enjoy family communion only through a TV soap opera. For the frustrated and frightened, it is an escape. Many desperate people, caught in a tightening vise of mounting economic and social pressures, find release in *The Carol Burnett Show*, *Flip Wilson* or *NFL* football. For most American children TV has become a primer on life.

Television cannot be brushed away as just another fad. It has sunk deep roots in the American heart and mind in a very short span of time.

TV seemed to plunk itself on the American scene just like another appliance. But it won acceptance almost immediately. It provided us with so much fun that we thought of it (and most of us still do) as a "plaything," a relatively inexpensive source of amusement and entertainment, never really questioning its capacity to influence human behavior, shape personalities, attitudes, and beliefs; we never bothered to find out if TV could be addictive. We accepted television on absolute faith. Before television was unveiled to the public, social scientists did not demand an opportunity from the physical scientists who developed TV to test how television would affect children psychologically and physiologically. Even during the past twenty-five years, while programs like *Combat, The Lone Ranger, Popeye, Road Runner, Love American Style, Beverly Hillbillies, The Rascals,* and soap operas plus commercials selling aspirins to zippers bombarded millions of children daily, there still was no outcry from the social science community for a serious investigation on the effects of television on young people. Their seeming lack of interest in researching TV's impact on humans indicates that most social scientists in the past two and a half decades evidently saw no correlation between televiewing and the rise in crime and violence, divorce, human insensitivity, social frustration, youth's disenchantment with school, youth's rebellion against authority, sexual promiscuity, and the emergence of the drug culture.

American psychology has virtually turned its back on television's influence on the child in the past twenty-five years. Meaningful studies in this area are extremely scarce. Out of a total of 145,319 abstracts published in

Psychological Abstracts[13] from 1962 to October 1972, only 37 dealt directly or indirectly with the effects of television on children. That means that in the past ten years only .02 percent of all of the psychological studies or articles published were devoted to TV's effect on kids.

The American medical community's record is no better. In his address to the American Academy of Pediatrics on October 17, 1971, Dr. Gerald Looney scolded his colleagues for their seeming lack of concern about the influence that television has on children. Dr. Looney cited the evidence: "The medical literature is almost devoid of articles on television, and most of the papers listed under the heading 'Television' in the catalog of topics for physicians and scientists, *The Cumulated Index Medicus,* describe mainly the medical and scientific applications of television and rarely mention content or effects.[14]

The Arizona Medical College professor explained to his fellow physicians why the medical community must participate actively in dealing with the medical problems that arise from children's relationship with television: "Because of the public's persistent and generally unquestioning faith in the medical profession, until physicians become part of the SOLUTION to the unknowns and uncertainties in children's television, they thereby must inevitably be considered part of the problem."[15]

For the most part educators have ignored the impact television has had on the human beings they are charged with educating. Colleges that produce teachers are not preparing their graduates to reach the television-influenced child. Most of those colleges operate as if television has had no effect, no influence on the lives of children. This is evidenced by the fact that not one university in New England, an area which traditionally

leads the nation in educational innovation, offers a
course on how to teach kids who are influenced by TV.

Why in the past twenty-five years have teachers and
professors of education not recognized this problem?
One could ask the psychologists, psychiatrists, and pediatricians the same question.

Basically, there is one overriding reason for their professional blindness in the area of TV and kids. They
simply have not taken television seriously. Many of them
consider TV a toy for children, an escape mechanism for
adults. Others see it as a "lowbrow" pleasure gadget and
feel that researching its effects on people would be like
researching the effects of ping pong on people. Some
have brushed aside the problem, because grant-offering
foundations and government agencies in the past have
not been interested in funding such projects. And there
have been those status-minded, insecure professionals,
who may have had an interest in dealing with the problem, but who shunned involvement for fear their colleagues would laugh at them.

But what TV may be doing to children is no joking
matter. And a few people in psychology, medicine, and
education are beginning to realize that. Their awakening
is due, in large measure, to the controversy raging over
the U.S. Surgeon General's study on the effects of televised violence on children, the success of *Sesame Street,*
and the tireless and courageous battle the organization
Action for Children's Television has waged to improve
and clean up the quality of children's television programming.

At a Yale University symposium on children and television, the overwhelming majority of social scientists,
physicians, educators, and communicators there were in
agreement that television is a major influence on the
lives of many American children. Their pronouncements

rang out with vigor, with concern, with a sense of urgency. But there were people at the symposium who reminded the psychologists, professors, and physicians of their past records. After a panel of distinguished scientists and early childhood education specialists completed their explanations as to why commercial TV kiddie programs and ads are bad for children, Lee Polk, an executive for ABC-TV's children's programming division asked the panel: "Where were you people during the past twenty-five years? We [the TV industry] could have used your help to structure healthy television programs for children."[16] Polk had jabbed a raw nerve.

Now is the time to make up for what was neglected in the past twenty-five years. Unity is needed. The networks, the local TV-station operators, the psychology, education, and medical communities and advertising specialists should cast aside their differences and prejudices and lock minds and hearts not only to make TV safe for children but to make it a means for their enlightenment. This unity should be based on a resolve to do everything in their power to understand television's capacity to hurt or help a viewer. In other words, to become more sensitive to TV's attributes. This unity should be expressed through a formal organization, represented by all of the concerned professional disciplines. The group should inspire, finance, and even engage in serious research, trying to determine scientifically exactly how television affects all segments of our society. What this organization unearths should be shared with the public so they can adjust their TV-viewing practices. The same information should be passed on to TV producers and used as a guide when putting programs together. For example, if research indicates that pictures showing children pulling a dog's tail sets off aggressive behavior in three- to five-year-olds, TV producers and their staffs

should know this and refrain from producing scenes like
that. And they should do the same if the traditional
cowboy and Indian scenes are found to reinforce racism.
They should internalize the research data, applying it to
what they produce. Once involved in this process, they
would develop a better appreciation for its need. To
achieve this kind of consciousness would require considerable purging of deeply rooted programming philosophy and production practices—not an easy task. But this
has to be done for the sake of the viewing audience.
Today there are entirely too many producers, writers,
and directors connected with programs who do not understand television's ability to teach what it shows, who
do not appreciate what their programs do to those who
are watching them. And tragically some who have an
inkling simply do not care. In most TV studios and film
and tape-editing rooms, the possibility of harming
viewers is rarely considered. Sam Sinclair Baker, a
former Madison Avenue advertising executive, pin-
points where the producers' main interests lie: "I've
worked with dozens of producers of children's shows and
with the personalities who appear as aunts, uncles,
clowns, and whatnots. They all had one thing in common: their overriding concern with how many sponsors
they could land and how many commercials they could
pack into each show. Some recognized their responsibility to try to make a program helpful and uplifting, but as a
strictly secondary consideration."[17]

Many of these producers and directors and writers are
experts in pushing the right buttons, pulling the right
levers, in putting together fast-paced dramatizations that
are technically flawless, not a second less or beyond the
prescribed length of the program. While they are working, their aim is to drive kids to the set and keep them
there, riveted to the message they designed. In a sense,

their approach and attitude is like that of an X-ray technician who works in an orderly, spotless room with smoothly functioning, expensive machinery and is unconcerned about exposing people to an overdose of radiation.

Television watchers, whether child or adult, should not be subjected to the producer's hunch or "Kentucky Wind" approach to creating programs. The producer and his staff should be sensitive to the potential effect their work would have on the audience; they should be prevented from rolling dice with human psyches.

Certainly research is not foolproof, but it could cut down the amount of poor behavior television teaches children. It would provide some guidance and meaningful restraint to producers who for too long operated on impulse, prejudice, and a desire to please the advertiser first.

The American people, I feel, are ready for the kind of TV-governing organization I propose, but those who control TV are not. The vested interest groups would resist such an establishment by condemning the concept as an infringement on freedom of expression and free enterprise, thus smokescreening from the public the far greater issue—television's damaging effect on children.

But there are a few bright spots in American television. The Children's Television Workshop, the producers of *Sesame Street,* is one; Family Communications, Inc., the producers of *Mister Rogers Neighborhood,* is another. At CTW the decision-making people are not afraid to scrap a production segment of *Sesame Street* or *Electric Company* if they feel it will hurt someone in their audience. The staff doesn't believe in sacrificing children for the sake of keeping its production budget in the black. "We have thrown out production pieces, which were ready to be aired," Pat Hayes, a researcher for *Sesame Street,* says, "because after viewing them we felt they would be harmful to the people we are trying to teach."

"The questionable ones," she adds, "are tested."

Pat Hayes and her colleagues are aware of the revenue loss connected with junking filmed or video-taped segments, but they are also aware of the damage television can cause to children if it is insensitively produced. Of course, CTW is not a wasteful organization. Heavy reliance on preproduction research and curriculum development helps to keep segment scrapping at a minimum. But more important, the research is a means of guarding against hurting the viewer. It helps in establishing what programs like *Sesame Street* and *Electric Company* should teach to their particular audiences and how the curriculum should be taught on TV. Much of the research is used to test the effectiveness of program segments. CTW spends $614,000 annually to carry out its research[18]—a healthy investment in human ecology, but something most producers of commercial children's TV would consider a terrible waste of money.

The organization that produces *Mister Rogers Neighborhood* is not structured like CTW, but the people who work on the show, like those at CTW, care about children. Tots between three and six who watch the program, know that, even though they are unable to articulate it. One of the reasons for the success of *Mister Rogers Neighborhood* is that producer/host Fred Rogers remembers how it feels to be a child. Achieving that awareness is a struggle. But he continually works at it, because he feels that is necessary in order to reach his TV audience. He can empathize with children. They know he knows their fears and bewilderments and how they feel when they are lonely, sad, or angry. He is an adult whom they can trust. *Mister Rogers Neighborhood* serves the child, never talking down to him or her, dealing with issues and episodes in life that other producers of children's TV programs would never dare touch. For example, during that tragic spring of 1968 when Dr. Martin Luther King, Jr., and Senator Robert Kennedy were assassinated, Rogers sensed that many families and children were taking these catastrophes personally. He pleaded with parents not to leave their children isolated and at the mercy of their own fantasies of loss and destruction, which tend to be much more frightening than any reality. On one program, he talked about death and grief in a way children could understand. On the Emmy citation for that particular program it is written that "Mister Rogers was the only one on television to think of the children's needs at this time of national mourning."[19]

Maybe the TV networks, independent television production firms, and free-lance producers could swallow their pride and adopt the programming approaches employed by the Children's Television Workshop and *Mister Rogers Neighborhood.* From this kind of exposure they might learn to appreciate the need for sensitivity in communicating to children, especially preschoolers, via television. They might begin to understand TV's power to teach what it shows.

One thing is certain; the present programming condition of commercial television—adult programming as well as children's programming—has to change. This is because many kids watch adult shows. It is unrealistic to think children confine their TV watching only to Saturday mornings. Weekday late afternoon is a popular time. So is early afternoon for preschoolers. Literally millions of children under twelve are still viewing television as late as ten o'clock on week nights.[20]

Obviously, parents have a responsibility to control televiewing in the home, to keep children away from adult programming that stresses violence, sex, sadism, or racism. The trouble is that many parents are not aware of this responsibility. Some become so engrossed in what they are watching that they are unable to detect any manifestation of antisocial behavior. Unfortunately, many who do, avoid making an issue of it for fear their child will throw a temper tantrum, keeping them from seeing whatever they are watching. There are those who simply see nothing wrong in allowing their children to watch whatever they want for as long as they wish. Even some conscientious parents cannot always be available to monitor their children's TV viewing. What it boils down to is that parents and children need help from the outside to control TV watching in the home. After all, parents are not perfect creatures; they make mistakes; they are unaware of many aspects of life; they have weaknesses. Parents need help, especially when it comes to protecting themselves and protecting their children from themselves. It is possible that unwise usage of television is as dangerous as unwise usage of heating gas or electricity. Some force outside the home—like a federal agency—is needed to prevent TV from causing deep psychological damage to our children's minds. It is unfair to children to subject them to television that most of the time portrays the seamier side of life, that models ugly, violent behavior, that makes cigar smoking a means to eternal happiness and a certain hair conditioner a guarantee of sexual dynamism. Something has to be done to clean up television, not only for our children's sake, but for society's sake, for today's children will have some say in the way our country runs in the future.

In many countries that have television, the kind of commercialism, violence, racism, sadism, and materialism that afflict the children's programs of our country would be prohibited. For example, when the television network of South Germany reviewed the American syndicated TV program *Speed Runner,* which is seen on many stations in the United States, it was banned not only from viewing by children but from viewing by adults as well. The German network officials felt the program was sadistic.[21] The National Citizens Committee for Broadcasting found in its survey of children's television in sixteen countries that in terms of sensitivity toward TV's impact on children, the United States was lagging behind almost every country studied. Many of those countries surveyed have open societies, so their television is not ruled by a totalitarian political regime which dictates what will or will not be aired. It is simply a case of their television policy makers and producers being more responsive to the needs of children, more sensitive to their fears, and more respectful of the power of the medium in which they work.

The survey disclosed, for example, that the United States was the only country that allows more commercials on children's programming than on adult evening television. Only four other countries studied permit advertising on children's programs. And they allow it for only eight minutes per hour, whereas in the United States it now averages twelve minutes per hour.[22] (Until January of 1973, the average was sixteen minutes. Only heavy pressure from groups like ACT forced many broadcasters to cut down on commercials on children's shows.)

The survey also showed that American children's shows are generally poor in content, relying heavily on cheaply produced cartoons that are aimed at a general audience from two to twelve years old.[23] Communicating responsibly to such a wide age span is extremely difficult when you consider the varied attention-span levels of the target audience and their levels of sophistication. Certainly, a twelve-year-old's interests are different from those of a two-year-old. U.S. producers tend to solve this problem by putting together shows that appeal to the basest instincts of humanity, stuff that excites and stimulates easily, slapstick comedy, haunted houses where monsters dwell, cowboys shooting Indians, wild chase scenes.

Unlike the United States, countries like Britain, Austria, Japan, West Germany, and Australia tailor their children's programs to specific age groups, for they are aware that what would be effective programming for one age level would not be for another.[24] What is pathetic is that American television is capable of doing what those countries are doing. We have manpower, the creativity, the technical expertise to do what they do. *Mister Rogers*, *Sesame Street* and *Electric Company* are classic examples of our capability to produce meaningful, sensitive, enriching children's television. But those shows are but a fraction of what is offered to American children on TV, and besides, they appear, for the most part, on public television, not commercial TV. What keeps commercial television from narrowing its audience aim? Greed. After all, the broader the audience, the bigger will be the advertisers' market.

The sorry state of television in the United States is not a new problem. It was 1961 that Newton Minow, then chairman of the Federal Communications Commission, delivered his famous "vast wasteland" indictment of TV programming. Little has been done to correct the situation between then and now. About the only area where there has been progress is in the number of people watching television and the number of hours each household has its set on. Actually, this kind of equation is hazardous when you consider the likely result of more people watching more of practically the same quality of television shown in 1961. If television is allowed to remain in its present state, we can, in the future, expect even more of the kind of program and commercial garbage that is fed our children today, simply because TV's appeal is growing. Imagine, with the spread of cable TV we will be exposed to more channels, which means more programs. Soon cable TV operators will be able to offer as many as fifty channels. In 1980, some communities will have eighty channels.[25] What kinds of programs will be on them? Will they be harmful to our children? These are questions that must be seriously considered. With more communications satellites in the sky we will be exposed to more programs from Africa, Asia, Australia, Europe, and Latin America. School children will be exposed to more instructional TV in the classroom and will be taking home video cassettes for homework instead of books. Kids will be watching more TV in the near future because there will be more of it, and one reason there will be more is that people will be demanding more. Obviously, quality and quantity control will be required, some kind of mechanism would have to be established that would help make television truly a culturally enriching experience for our people and, at the same time, keep video garbage from polluting the minds of our children.

3

A Look at
American TV through
Unprejudiced Eyes

Television is so popular, so accessible, that it can easily mesh with the rhythm of our home life. When that happens, we become so emotionally involved with TV that it becomes part of the family's pattern of life. That kind of entanglement makes it difficult for most people to be objective about TV.

It takes someone who is not emotionally involved with television, but who understands its nature, is sensitive to its qualities and potentialities and who has not seen much of it for a while to make a fair assessment of it. Dr. Richard Andre, who has been consulting and teaching at Brazil's Institute of Space Research, possesses those qualifications. For two years he and his family were in Brazil, where they saw very little TV. After a three-month trip to the United States, where he saw lots of television, Dr. Andre made this assessment of American video fare:

"In October of 1972 my family and I made a return trip to the U.S. This occasion provided us with the opportunity to regain some of the cultural comfort that we had known for our entire lives before going to Brazil. This included seeing American television again. We were actually looking forward to this experience, especially with respect to the educational programming for children. Our son, Jalal, was now two and one-half years old and had been demonstrating his capacity to be a sponge in soaking up new and stimulating learning experiences. We soon discovered that he was a natural TV child and he soon wanted to eat his breakfast with his highchair parked in front of the television while the morning children's programs were finding their way into his receptive mind. This seemed to be quite beneficial and we were able to easily recognize the beneficial potentials of television.

"Occasionally, Jalal would convince us that he was not tired and therefore should be permitted to stay up at night in order to watch some special program. I should admit that we encouraged this because some of the best children's specials were programmed for 8:00 or 8:30 P.M. At the termination of one such program, a series episode of a "district attorney" type police drama began in a way that caught us completely by surprise—so much so, that we were all captivated and carried off into a scene of intense drama without our awareness of what was taking place. The set was a room where a man and a woman were involved in a situation of severe verbal abuse. Before the audience had an opportunity to comprehend what was going on, the woman screamed, 'Don't kill me! Put down that gun! Please don't shoot!' Then a shot rang out and a circle of blood saturated the woman's dress as she fell to the floor.

"At that moment I realized that Jalal was still in the room and his eyes told me that he was horrified—shocked—distraught and confused by what he had just witnessed. Then I realized that this was his first television murder and its effect made me intensely conscious of what a powerful medium television is. I was also angry at the human damage that had taken place—angry at myself for not realizing sooner what was going on—angry at an industry that makes a major portion of its profit from the dissemination of moral decadence and angry at the society that has permitted such universal diseases as violence to spread unchecked and unattended.

"I realize that to merely condemn the television industry or for that matter, society, for such flagrant and manipulative misuse of this powerful medium would be dysfunctional and irresponsible. What is needed is to recognize the inherent power of television and to educate the industry and the society so that they utilize the power that television commands in order to benefit and uplift man rather than glorify his decadence. An example of how this can be and is being accomplished was demonstrated in another television series which we were fortunate enough to see while we were in the U.S.

"The series is called 'The Curiosity Shop' and although we only saw this program once during our stay, I am quite certain the producers of the series are in tune with the human needs of kids. The show is built around a very beautiful human trait called 'curiosity' which is something that children instinctively seem to manifest. They want to learn, to discover all that there is to know. In the most fascinating segment of the program a little boy was at first curious about how big, how vast the universe is. So a kind of animated telescoping camera took over and the television carried its audience off on a tremendous voyage through the vastness of time and space. First one saw the boy in a boat, then as we moved away, the boy and the boat became a dot on a lake, then the lake merged into the land and water mass of the Great Lakes region, then that region became lost in a continent,

and then lost again in a hemisphere. A curved horizon
line came into view, then a sphere that we know of as
Earth. Jupiter and Saturn whizzed by, then the sun—all
became lost as the tiny dot of our solar system was
engulfed in a large mass of stars, each one representing a
separate solar system. A galaxy then loomed into view
and then it even became a tiny dot as we entered another
galaxy. Then all merged into the vast blackness of the
universe. Then the camera reversed and speeded up as
we returned to the curiosity shop through a microscoping process. But it did not stop when we returned to the
relative reality of the human plane of existence. The
microscoping camera focused inward on the boy's arm
where a tiny mosquito was beginning to bite. The smooth
skin gave way to pores and mountains as the camera
continued to take us on a journey into the micro-universe.
Ordered systems of cells whizzed by and soon molecular
structures came into view like some unknown city of the
future. The camera went still further and soon we found
ourselves within a universe that was as limitless as the
one we had visited in the macro-world of existence. It
was time to return to the world of the human senses and
so the camera reversed itself and again sped up so that we
saw and were able to comprehend the importance of our
journey. The universe was that which encompassed all
that we could comprehend or perceive outwardly or
inwardly. And further, the message was the same at
either extreme—that the universe is an ordered system
that inherently manifests integrity, unity, and oneness
and that we as human beings are given the bounty of
being able to comprehend all the knowledge that the
universe has to offer.

"We had sat spellbound in a state of wonderment and
fascination. This was a profound demonstration of what
television has to offer. It can be a dynamic vehicle for

facilitating the development and release of human potential or it can remain the equally powerful instrument of
human destruction and degradation that it presently
more often is. The direction in which man takes all of his
technology is very simply a matter of his individual and
collective volition—it's a question of will."

4

The Child: A TV Target

Television is an instrument that transmits messages. The targets for its messages are human beings, young and old. It is not partial to age; anyone who watches is TV's target. Whether people comprehend the intended message is another matter. But even if the viewer does not fully understand a TV message, he usually perceives something from being exposed to it. Exactly what, is difficult to determine. But we do know that a child's TV viewing affects his behavioral development.

A child becomes a television target every time he turns on a TV set. What he is riddled with depends on what he watches. Of course, parents do not view their children as a target of television simply because they do not understand the nature of television. They consider TV a fun thing that keeps children out of mischief. In a sense, every time parents allow their children to watch whatever they wish and for as long as they wish, they are gambling with the health of their children.

It is important that parents understand that television is a powerful means of communication that regularly hits its targets—all human beings. Parents should also know

45

that the younger a child is, the more penetrable he is as a target. A child comes into our world helpless, a tender being, vulnerable to the effects of his environment. When he reaches adulthood, he represents the highest form of living creation on earth. But his journey from birth to manhood is a perilous adventure. How he evolves depends, in large measure, on his parents' care. An uncaring, unloving, self-centered adult is usually the product of a home environment composed of parents who are uncaring, unloving, and self-centered. Parents who are careless, who are half-hearted, who simply go through the motions in caring for their children—these parents tend to produce children who are emotionally scarred. Often these scars are not visible in public. They gnaw quietly at the psyche, generating neurosis and paranoia. Even well-meaning, conscientious parents who are ignorant of how to aid their children's development make many mistakes which affect the way the children mature as human beings.

A child is not to be taken lightly or taken for granted. He is a human being that requires great care and more attention than an adult—just as a sapling needs more care than a fully grown tree. He is a tender, evolving, potentially intelligent creation with a questing instinct and a natural urge to grow. The infant's search for his mother's breast is an expression of that urge. The yearning for a close embrace is another way infants express their desire to grow. When an infant struggles to reach an object that fascinates him, his curiosity is aroused, he wants to know, and discovering cultivates his growth process.

A child comes into our world wanting to grow. It is his parents' obligation to make certain that the child's growth is not warped, that the child fulfills his growth capacity as a human being. If a woman and a man are conscientious parents, they will view their parental responsibility as a serious challenge, a deeply creative undertaking, because they will understand that the destiny of their child depends in large measure on the way they care for him. It is a tough job, because they must concern themselves with not only the physical survival of their child but his emotional, intellectual, and spiritual development as well. It is not an eight-hour, five-day-a-week responsibility. It is the most sensitive human challenge. It can also be a deeply rewarding experience, especially when parents see the fruit of their labor enter the world as a strong, loving individual equipped to fulfill himself and to serve society wholeheartedly, meaningfully.

A child is learning all of the time. His home is his first school; his parents are his first teachers. Besides discovering their child's potentialities, parents must provide a home environment whereby those potentialities can be released and recognized by the child. The environment must also help the child to develop a strong self-concept, emotional strength, and an appreciation and motivation for serving his family and community.

Caring parents try to expose their child to experiences that would stimulate his intellectual, social, and emotional development. On the other hand, caring parents make certain that the environment they create does not damage him psychologically and physiologically. They keep him from playing with rifles and pistols and knives; steer him away from broken glass; keep pornography from him; try to keep him from experiencing acts of violence or racist talk and behavior.

But even caring parents make mistakes in creating a healthy home environment for their children. They make a mistake when they fail to consider television a part of their children's home environment. They are guilty of an oversight that could hurt their sons' and daughters' growth pattern. It could undo all of the good feeling, the good habits, established in the home. The smut, the violence, the racism, the sadism, the sexism their children see on television could cancel out the efforts of parents to protect their children from experiencing anti-social behavior in other family activities.

If today's parents are concerned about the healthy development of their children, they *must* seriously consider television an important part of their home environment. Eliminating TV in the home won't help, because children can watch it with other children in the neighborhood. And TV is the dominating medium of the day. Kids talk about it, are influenced by it. Parents must be sensitive to the peer pressure their children face in school and on the street. Besides, why deny a child the good that TV provides?

In incorporating TV in the home environment, parents must understand how it could influence their children for good or bad. For the same reason that parents make a concerted effort to provide healthy and wholesome food for their family, they should strive to learn how to control television use in the home and to distinguish between worthwhile and harmful TV. They should always remember that when their child sits before a TV set, he is a target for TV.

5

It's Real to a Child

Little four-year-old Suzie is seated on the floor, closer to the TV set than where her mother placed her to watch *Mr. Rogers Neighborhood.* She had actually been placed in a chair, but as the program progressed she slipped down to the floor and began inching toward the set. Suzie is unaware of her journey from the chair to a spot only two feet from the big pulsating TV tube. She is too busy interacting with Mr. Rogers to make note of where she ended up sitting. Her involvement with Mr. Rogers draws her to the set—for her a perfectly natural social reflex. Two people who like each other, she believes, like to be close to each other! For Suzie, the experience with Mr. Rogers is real; he comes to her house as a friend, always on time, always creating fun and making her happy. Suzie believes he likes her; he tells her this everyday—not only with words—but by the way he treats her, by the way he looks at her; in her mind they are linked. Unfortunately, Suzie's mother and father are not conscious of the intensity of their daughter's friendship with Mr. Rogers. They feel Suzie simply sits passively, being entertained while exposed to television. If they

would take the time to observe their little girl experiencing TV, they would most likely learn that, at times, she
talks back to her TV friends, gives them advice and will
respond to a TV character's farewell by waving her hand
and crying out, "Goodbye!"

Suzie may be an imaginary character, but her actions
before the set are fairly typical of thousands of children
across our country. Preschoolers believe that the TV
characters they consider their friends are real, not actors.
In fact, many children are certain that the television
personalities they love know who they are and where
they live. Some *Sesame Street* personnel have noticed
this kind of behavior in young children. Dr. Edward
Palmer, vice-president and director of research for Children's Television Workshop, the producers of *Sesame
Street*, shared with a university audience in England two
years ago a few observations that bear this out: "Most
children believe the [Sesame Street] cast members really are the people they see on TV, and that they really do
live on Sesame Street. They have little conception of
'actors.' Furthermore, a good many children are convinced that the cast knows them as well as they know the
cast. One viewer was very indignant when Bob McGrath
(a regular program character) asked where he (the child)
lived. The little boy replied, 'You know where I live.
You're there everyday.' "[1]

Social scientists at Yale University's Child Study
Center have had similar experiences. Katherine R. Lustman, the co-director of the center's nursery school, has
observed: "Day after day one sees them [children] imitating bizarre behavior of the characters in these programs [*Batman, Superman, Gigantor, Star Trek* and
Lost in Space] and not getting any closer to understanding the pretend quality or what they were all about.
Indeed, it took a good deal of their energy and it was

almost impossible for the adults to clarify the situations they played out. I remember asking one child, 'Are Batman and Robin real or pretend?' and his shocked response, 'Oh, no, they're really real.' "[2]

Television characters and episodes aren't considered real only by American young children. There are plenty of kids in Japan, Brazil, Germany, Britain, the Philippines, and many other countries who react to TV the way their American counterparts do.

Former Peace Corps volunteer Linda Meyers noticed this while working in Medellin, Colombia, from 1965 to 1967:

"Children watching educational television programs in Colombia reacted to the TV teacher as if she were actually physically present in the classroom, that is, they stood up and called out good morning when she came on the air, waved goodbye to her at the end of the program and vied anxiously with each other to answer the questions she asked during the program. The younger children took for granted that she could see them. (Older children were more skeptical and often asked, 'She can't really see us, can she?')

"Classroom teachers were advised to encourage the children to answer the TV teacher's questions, and there was usually a great flurry of waving arms and snapping fingers (the Colombian school child's way of indicating that he knows the answer).

"It was interesting to watch what happened when the second-grade math teacher decided to 'personalize' her question asking by using a child's name at the end of each question, thus indicating that José or Maria should respond. I recall seeing one little boy named Francisco so overwhelmed by being singled out of his class of sixty to seventy children that he could scarcely stand up—much less find words to answer the question.

"It didn't take long, however, for the second graders to resolve the question of whether or not they could actually be seen by the TV teacher. Because Colombia schools are segregated by sex, the teacher used boys' names during one program and girls' names the next. At first, the children were puzzled: 'Why does she call on Roberto when we are all girls?' Even when the truth dawned, however, it didn't seem to make much difference: dozens of arms still waved and fingers snapped and voices cried out, 'I know, I know.'"

Could it be that the second graders in that Colombian school accepted intellectually that the TV teacher was not in their classroom but emotionally felt she was there? Certainly the way they kept responding to her questions is a strong indication that that was the case.

Even some adults accept what TV offers as reality, more quickly than if they experienced the same thing in the street. A classic example of this is the way Richard Speck, the convicted murderer of eight student nurses, realized what he had done. In his autobiography, Speck recalls that while still at large in Chicago, more than a week after he had committed the crime, he looked up at a TV set in a tavern and saw the face of O.W. Wilson, superintendent of police, saying: "We're looking for a man named Richard Speck." At that instant, Speck writes, he knew he had committed the murders.[3]

With many children, television is as necessary as sleeping and eating. From the cradle they have been immersed in TV and nourished by its messages. It has always been in the house, they reason, just like the water faucet, bathtub, or refrigerator—a natural part of their home environment. In fact, in most cases, TV was in the home before they were. Children are creatures of television and feel life would be meaningless without it. For some kids it is even a necessary stimulant for their unconscious mind. That was dramatically reinforced for me when one of the professors at the University of Massachusetts, Dr. Juan Caban, related an experience he had in one of his classes in the spring of 1972: "A doctoral student in education, an outspoken opponent of television, revealed an encounter he had with a four-year-old boy concerning television watching. When he told the child that he did not watch TV and that he did not own a TV set, the youngster appeared bewildered and said, 'That's terrible, then you must never dream.' "

Parents make a mistake of pooh-poohing the reality of the relationship their preschool child has with characters on TV. Because a parent cannot believe that his child can accept a TV character as a real friend or a television episode as a real experience does not mean that what his child experiences watching TV is not real to him. Too often parents allow their own prejudices, attitudes, and beliefs to cloud their perception of their own children. They even project their own feelings and tastes onto their children, a practice that stunts the development of a child's individuality and can set off an unconscious hate of his parents, a feeling which can surface when he is older.

When a parent notices his child acting like Suzie in front of a TV set, he should view that as a sign that his child considers his TV experience real. But a parent's acceptance of this situation should be no reason for him to panic. It should, however, compel the mother or father to check carefully what the child watches, lest he develop an admiring relationship with a chap portraying a swindler or drug addict on a certain soap opera he watches regularly with an older person. On the other hand, relationships with *Sesame Street*'s Oscar or Susan would be acceptable. So would Captain Kangaroo, Mr. Greenjeans, Bill Cosby on *Electric Company,* or Fred

Rogers. In other words, children should be allowed to develop "real" relationships with TV characters. In time they will grow to know the truth. What is important, however, is that parents make certain their children's TV relationships are with wholesome characters.

The chances that a child will grow into an adult still consciously believing that Oscar and Popeye are real is extremely remote. As the child grows, his understanding of reality grows. He is better equipped to distinguish between reality and unreality. When most children reach the age of ten or eleven, they seem to understand intellectually that the characters they see dancing on television are not aware of them or the thousands, possibly millions, of other viewers. They seem to understand intellectually that the TV dancers are in a studio located perhaps thousands of miles away, performing before a battery of cameras.

Though studies indicate that older children are more sophisticated TV viewers, are more selective of programming, and more skeptical of TV commercial claims, the fact remains that these same children were once preschoolers, open, gullible, impressionable little human beings absorbing all—the good and bad—of TV for five straight years; most of them spending, according to Neilsen Television Index, fifty-four hours a week before the set. Certainly, what they took in was not erased when the candles on their sixth birthday cake were blown out. There is evidence that everything humans perceive is stored in their brains,[4] that perceptions affect people's behavioral pattern even if they cannot remember them.

I feel that what a young adult perceived through television during his first five years of life and the years that followed are interrelated, that what he learned at three, four, and five through TV affects the shaping of his personality and influences his behavior as an adult. What was accepted as reality at the age of five was woven into the complicated tapestry of impressions, effects, and knowledge accumulated over the years, becomes a vibrant factor in the activity of the subconscious mind, and influences human behavior. In simpler terms, there is "a little bit of the kid" in all adults—the result of the influences, perceptions, and experiences humans have been exposed to before they reached maturity.

Long before TV, Plato warned about the impressionability of the young, open mind of a child: "The young are not able to distinguish what is and what is not allegory, but whatever opinions are taken into the mind at that age are wont to prove indelible and unalterable."[5]

Even if parents reject the theory that preschoolers accept TV experiences as real experiences, there is considerable evidence that television stimulates children to action. A lot of the evidence can be found in the average American home. Thousands of kids see a show and rush outside to create a game based on the program they've just watched, or the more impatient might create and play a game in the living room. There are other times when a child might wait an hour, even a day, possibly two days before carrying out an urge that was triggered by a certain TV episode or personality. With some children, I feel, the daily dose of TV accumulates, not sparking immediate action. Sometimes months, even years, can elapse without anything happening. But the TV exposure mounts in some kids, the way a bucket collects water from a melting icicle, drop by drop. Eventually, the water runs over.

Back in the fifties, during TV's infancy, I remember seeing boys playing Hopalong Cassidy, riding imaginary horses and chasing imaginary outlaws. The more resourceful fellow played a dual role, both cowboy and horse. He was cowboy from the waist up and horse from the waist down. When he'd break into a gallop, the cowboy part would whack the horse part, urging the horse to move faster. And there were the neighborhood Tarzans who would swing down from trees on makeshift "jungle vines," crying out, in high soprano, Tarzan's blood-curdling call. You knew when the most conscientious kid Tarzan swung into action, because he usually wore a bathing suit.

In the sixties, I remember two of my sons—they were four and five then—battling over who would play the role of Daniel Boone. When they settled their argument, I would find them crawling on the floor, wearing coonskin caps, carrying broomsticks as rifles and about to pounce on an imaginary enemy.

Today, kids simulate space adventures and take imaginary trips to the moon and different planets; they take turns playing their Saturday cartoon heroes or pretend to be a zoomer. They practice swinging a bat the way Hank Aaron swings on TV or passing a football the way Joe Namath passes it. On the Little League baseball fields, you find kids hitching up their pants and pulling the peaks of their caps the way they have seen the pros do it on TV.

Not all of the TV-induced backyard or playground escapades end happily. Some of the skinny kids playing Tarzan literally knock the breath out of themselves by beating their chests with their fists. When Lash LaRue was a favorite TV hero, many parents bought Lash LaRue whips for their children and the kids would engage in whip duels, causing playground casualties. Zoro fans whirled whips rather freely also, snapping open the skin of many a youngster. A psychology professor and colleague of mine remembers when his nephew, playing Superman, tied a towel around his neck, tried to fly from his mother's dresser to his bed, and missed, cracking his collarbone. There have been cases where children have tried to hang themselves after seeing a hanging dramatized on television.

"In March, 1964, Michael Lee Gambril, a nineteen-year-old Marine on leave, reported that after watching a horror movie on TV, 'something came over him' which caused him to kill his father, mother and sister with a hatchet."[6]

In October 1973 Boston police blamed a TV movie for a bizarre murder in their city. A gang of youths poured gasoline over a woman and set her ablaze. The murder method was featured in *Fuzz*, a movie on ABC two nights before the woman was killed. During the same month this grizzly scene was reenacted in Miami, Flordia. Two thirteen-year-olds and a twelve-year-old were charged with first-degree murder.[7]

TV stimulates less physical action also, which can be deadly. For example, television has glorified pill popping, conditioning children to rely on pills to cure what ails them, to make them more powerful, bigger, more alert, smarter, more beautiful, and happier. After all, kids repeatedly see pills driving away nasty hammers in people's skulls, lightning bolts shooting into human spines, and sharp-beaked gremlins picking away at stomach linings. They have seen how grouchy, sour-looking people turn fresh, sweet, and charming in less than thirty seconds by swallowing a pill. For many children, especially preschoolers, a pill performs miracles.

Four-year-old Erin Shelton of Overland Park, Kansas—who like many other little boys dreams of being strong—was so impressed by a vitamin-pill commercial on *Captain Kangaroo* that when he found the advertised brand of pills in his mother's grocery bag, he took the bottle, opened it, and swallowed forty pills, thinking the more you take the stronger you become. But Erin nearly died. He was rushed to the hospital, suffering from both vitamin A and iron poisoning. At the hospital his stomach was pumped and he was fed intravenous fluid and placed in intensive care, where he hovered between life and death for forty-eight hours.[8]

With some children television has a way of stimulating them to copy certain practices and actions they see on the tube. They'll even try to see if it works at home or elsewhere in the neighborhood. In Los Angeles, for example, a housemaid caught a seven-year-old boy sprinkling broken glass into his family's stew. He did it not because he disliked his family, but because he wanted to see if it would work the way it worked on television. In Syracuse, a fourteen-year-old boy who is fascinated with electronics used the techniques he saw on *Mission Impossible* to commit a number of robberies. He was caught only because a friend notified the authorities.[9]

Television even stimulates adults to action. The Federal Aviation Administration knows that. In 1971 the FAA urged TV stations around the country not to show the film *The Doomsday Flight* because the agency felt the movie was responsible for a surge in telephoned bomb threats to airlines. The film is about a plot to extort money from an airline by claiming that an explosive aboard a certain flight would go off if the plane descends below a particular altitude. Money is demanded in return for information as to where the bomb is located. The FAA pointed out that "the number of anonymously telephoned bomb threats received by local airlines rose significantly" each time *The Doomsday Flight* was shown. At least two flights, the agency added, were interrupted as a result of similar threats made soon after the movie appeared on TV.[10]

Most TV advertisers know that television stimulates children to act, and their commercials are engineered to have the kids act the way they want them to act—as their unpaid salesmen. The Davy Crockett craze of 1955 was evidence of this. Three hundred Davy Crockett products were produced, luring $300 million from American parents.[11] In most cases it was the TV-titillated child who persuaded his parents to dig into their pockets for Davy Crockett coonskin caps, moccasins, sweatshirts, books, records, and candy.

The need for recognition is a major reason why children imitate their heroes. They need recognition because it provides them with confidence, and confidence is a necessary ingredient to the healthy development of a human being. The internal pull for recognition is so great that even young children who have no real-flesh friends will try to impress their imaginary companions often with feats learned from their TV heroes.

Children imitate a lot of what they see on TV. Dr. Gerald S. Lesser, a professor at Harvard's Laboratory for Human Development, who is *Sesame Street*'s chief advisor, has observed that children have a tendency to imitate what they see on television. "Our early observations of children watching television contained innumerable instances of specific modeling. It became obvious that children frequently imitate the physical motions of televised characters. When Sesame Street cast members count on their fingers or use their fingers or other parts of the body to shape letters or forms, many children copy them . . . . If a character on television does something absurd, such as stepping in a bucket, children will get up and pretend to walk around with buckets on their feet, too."[12]

Children tend to imitate those TV characters they admire. It stands to reason that the kinds of behavior models children are exposed to on television depend on what programs they watch.

Where there is no quality TV-viewing control in a home, the chances are greater that children will imitate more antisocial behavior because their TV heroes are characters who overcome evil with a fist or gun or who always triumph because of their ability to deceive and charm.

Banning TV in the home won't stifle a child's urge to imitate people he admires. He'll find heroes elsewhere, perhaps his father, his brothers, or the man or woman down the block. To a child, imitating the behavior of those he respects is a natural instinct. The wise parent will find the healthy models on TV and expose his child to them. But even wise parents cannot always prevent their children from being exposed to poor models. Mrs. Jane Grover of Petersham, Massachusetts, has a daughter who enjoys making up and acting out sexy commercials—a result, she feels, of her child's exposure to poor models on TV: "We are quite selective about our children's television watching. However, we cannot control the ads they watch! Allison, who is nine years old, has been making up and putting on TV ads during her playtime lately. She uses Basic H, a liquid vegetable base cleaner which is never advertised either on TV or in magazines. She demonstrates the extraordinary cleaning powers of this product on stove, refrigerator and walls. All this is done in a sexy voice and in a provocative manner, à la 'Serta mattress' or panty hose ads—or Barbie doll ads, for example."

David Lubin, now a doctoral candidate at Harvard's Graduate School of Education, liked television as a child. It helped structure his concept of reality. In fact, a number of his TV heroes reinforced his wish to become a lawyer. But what he accepted as reality as a child and even as a youth clashed with what reality actually is. When he went out in the world, he learned that TV had misled him: "Like most of my friends I needed heroes. You know, someone a kid can count on to be strong, brave, smart and successful—someone to be like when one grows up. Unlike many, I was not a sports addict, so I turned to television characters as a vent for my worship. This, combined with a strong desire to be a lawyer, made demigods of such greats as Perry Mason, and my heroes in *Judd for the Defense, The Defenders* and *The Bold Ones.* "How often I saw myself seated in a flashy convertible car with my Della Street beside me, rushing to the aid of my innocent client just accused of murder in the first degree; and then again in the courtroom bringing the real murderer to his knees in front of the teary-eyed jury. Yes, this was the reality of being a lawyer. It was easy to believe, all of the lawyers I had ever seen in action were like this. Of course, all of them were on television.

"Then at the end of my junior year in college I had the chance to go to Washington, D.C., and work in the U.S. Commission on Civil Rights. Here I would surely see my heroes in action. I'd heard the commission was loaded with bright, zealous young Ivy League lawyers. I looked forward to this warm-up session, thinking how great it would be someday when I was a lawyer.

"After the novelty wore off in about two weeks, I began to be confronted with information I was totally unable to understand. My 'heroes' spent their day nose down and head deep in dusty old books or writing often foolish memoranda from one office to the next, or on the telephone with the guy who didn't fix the plumbing correctly or didn't meet some contract on time, and on, and on, and on. This was a reality alien to me. Where was the romance, intrigue, investigation, suspense and glory? Where were my heroes? After several long talks with the fallen gods, I realized I'd been tricked: no one goes to court these days; lawyers don't always seek justice; making the best deal is all that counts; Della Street is more likely a fifty-year-old, graying woman; and much of the lawyer's day is spent doing dull, boring, tedious labor. Television had spoonfed me a reality so unlike the one I found in Washington, D.C., I just didn't know what to think or who to believe.

"After I returned home six weeks later, I did know who to believe and it was a sad experience. As I walked in the door of my home my mother greeted me with her usual warmth and all I could say was, 'Ma! They lied to me.'"

6

What Many Kids
Can't Have

George Wallace, campaigning for the Democratic presidential nomination, swept into Maryland as buoyant and blunt talking as ever. He was tasting a primary victory in that state. The crowds he drew were warm, enthusiastic, and big. But Wallace's campaigning dash came to an abrupt halt one afternoon in a Maryland shopping center. A clean-cut-looking young man with a pistol lunged from the crowd of Wallace admirers and fired several shots at the Alabama governor. Wallace fell to the ground, clutching his abdomen. Seconds later, the assailant, Arthur Bremer, was on the ground being pummeled by people around him. Bremer, who offered no resistance, was finally rescued by the police.

What led the twenty-one-year-old unemployed Milwaukee youth to try to murder Governor Wallace? No one knows the complete answer. But a look at his home life and school experience provides some insights. Arthur Bremer came from an uneducated poor family. His parents argued and fought continuously, and quite often over Arthur. The father felt his wife wasn't feeding Arthur and the other children enough. The mother treated

Arthur harshly, often beating him. He grew to dislike her. In school, Arthur was a poor student. But during his senior year in high school, he flashed some writing ability in a theme he wrote in English class, for which he received an "A." Though the main character of the composition is a boy named Paul, the theme is autobiographical. Midway, the theme turns to reflections on "Paul's" home life:

"In all the families on television, the mother was a pretty, high school graduate and never thought of not feeding her kids meals. The mothers of television always smiled at their kids and kissed their foreheads. My mother did not kiss me. She would not say 'hello' to me after I came into the house from school.

"I used to hate those television mothers. Now I hate Mom. I dreamed about Donna Reed, my television mother, cooking dinner for me and kissing my forehead.

"If Dad were only married to Donna Reed! Man!

"Dad was all right. He drove a lousy truck for a living. I thought he would be happy with Donna Reed. Dad did not have many friends. He only had Mom. So he would not leave her no matter what. I remember how he would come home after work. He would be tired and have a hungry gut. He would complain that Mom was not feeding my younger brother or him or me. Mom would shout. Dad would swear, and my younger brother would cry. Mom and Dad threw things at each other. I could hear them even though I was in the bedroom and my pillow was over my ears. I tried to think about pretty Donna Reed while Dad shouted and swore.

"I liked to think that I was living with a television family and there was no yelling at home, and no one hit me . . . ."[1]

Television was a factor in shaping Arthur Bremer's

outlook on life, his behavior. His TV experience was more than a dream, because he could see Donna Reed week after week. A dream comes quickly and goes quickly. But a TV series can last a long time. Every time Arthur Bremer clicked on his set to see Donna Reed, his feelings for her were reinforced. But while his love for his television mother grew, so did his frustration with his home life. Donna Reed was not going to crawl out of the TV set and replace his natural mother in his family's rundown flat in Milwaukee.

There are many children in our country who are experiencing the kind of frustration Bremer experienced by watching TV. Many of them, like Bremer, live in substandard housing in deteriorating neighborhoods. Television is their only periscope to the world. They see kids their age on family-type programs living in big beautiful homes, graced by the latest electrical appliances, two automobiles, a basketball play area, pets, and parents who love each other, always smiling, kind, considerate, understanding, and available for comforting when sadness strikes their children. That kind of tantalizing can be cruel, because through TV a poor child can always see what he likes but knows he cannot have. He begins to wonder, "Why do other kids have good things, happy lives, and fun times and I don't?" As he grows older and recognizes that he is as far away from the social paradise portrayed on television as he was when he was younger, he becomes hostile, hating the society that creates and fosters such social inequity, hating his parents for not giving him what the kids on TV have, and hating himself for not being able to break out of his trap.

During the racial riots of the late sixties, many frightened and angry whites wondered why American blacks were so dissatisfied with their lot when they had finally won their civil rights through legislation. Many of those who asked that question when Watts, Newark, and Detroit were burning are still baffled.

Television was a factor in igniting the hate that drove some blacks to the torch and the Molotov cocktail. These blacks watched TV and saw what the American dream was and what it was like to have fulfilled it. They wanted to turn that dream into reality for themselves. They wanted to be able to buy the things their children saw advertised on TV and desired.

"Television has had a more revolutionary impact on the inner city ghetto than any other part of American life," Brandeis University Professor Max Lerner claims. "Through the TV set, he [the black] sees the larger society. And what does he see? He sees Babylonian surfaces of life. He sees the opulence of it. And if he were not sufficiently convinced of the opulence by what he sees in the ordinary shows on TV, the commercials convince him . . . . He stretches out his hands to this opulent, sensual, affluent society wanting to get some of it instantly and it recedes. Like Tantalus, of the Greek myth, he stretches out his hands and the opulence recedes—and the result is rage."[2]

Television not only frustrates the economically deprived viewer, but it can turn that frustration into hate, which grows the more he watches TV. In 1966 a young Vista volunteer, Douglas Ruhe, witnessed that process in action while living with a poor family in Oregon:

"The people I was assigned to were considered 'hard core' welfare recipients. They were of French ancestry. The father was 95 percent disabled, a hard drinker and avowed cynic. His work used to be sport fishing. The mother was a veteran migrant worker, born in or near an apple orchard in the Wilamentic valley and raised on the road, moving from crop to crop.

"In the evening the father and mother and their three

children and any guests that were around would gather around the battered little TV set in the living room. And, unlike most viewers I have seen before or since, would become involved in a dialogue with the TV characters on the programs and advertisements.

"The father was plainly the leader of the dialogue. He particularly hated commercials which portrayed Americans as smiling, affluent, happy types. Often he would jeer at the sales pitch and curse the people on the screen. The rest of the family, including the children, would add invective, even throw refuse at the screen and mock the actors' smiles and remarks."

The America that those people saw on TV, and could not have, had become their enemy.

It is cruel to show people who dwell in slums—day after day—what it is like to live in comfort, never having to worry about heat in the winter, clean water, enough food to eat, and hungry rats. Of course, the television people who produce the programs that tease, that frustrate, that anger the poor do not think of themselves as misanthropes bent on wounding the poor of our society. In fact, many of them may consider themselves advocates of social progress. The trouble is, when they produce shows, they do not concern themselves with the impact, the harm, their effort will have on the poor. While in the TV studio, they do not think of the misery of slum dwellers or the social wretchedness of the rural poor. But the themes of idyllic Americana they create cross the minds of the teased, the frustrated, the angry in the Chicano ghetto of San Antonio, in Harlem, in Appalachia, and in hundreds of other communities where there are no telephones, dishwashers, washing machines, or indoor toilets, where the only link with the outside world is the TV set.

But while television accidentally pains the poor, it

accidentally helps them too. Television has helped the
poor to appreciate the magnitude of their plight, the
social injustice to which they have been subjected. It has
helped to break that ancient fatalistic hold on them—that
nothing can shake them free from the fetters of poverty,
that it is their destiny to be poor. Now, more ghetto poor
aspire to something better. Some who meet resistance
will scream, claw, even punch for the opportunity to
build the kind of life they have seen on TV shows like *My
Three Sons, Leave It to Beaver, The Brady Bunch* and
The Partridge Family.

In the past twenty-five years, the glowing, almost sanc-
tified picture painted of the average American family by
family-type TV shows has hurt middle-class kids also.
Their families may have two cars, the latest electrical
appliances, pets, and a basketball hoop on the garage, but
they are families not free of serious problems. In the best
of homes today children and parents clash, husbands and
wives argue—sometimes bitterly—and people do things
that Amy Vanderbilt might disapprove of. Though showing emotion, losing one's composure, making a mistake
are temporary human flaws, many children do not see
television parents with such defects. And they are very
much aware of the difference in behavior. That awareness grows with the amount of TV the child watches. For
many children, television establishes the standard for
how they think their parents should act. When their
parents continually fall short of the standard, the children
lose respect for them. A communications gap develops
between child and parents, and the home with two cars,
fancy appliances, and many other material niceties becomes a family battleground, leaving the parent wonder-
ing, "What went wrong?"

Television has not only frustrated many children, it has
also made them impatient. They are conditioned to ob-

taining instant pleasure. One common way is by turning on the TV set, their primary source of pleasure. All it takes is the pushing of a button or the turning of a knob and—zap!—their favorite program is on.

They are accustomed to seeing solutions to even the most complex problems arrived at quickly. In a detective episode, for example, children experience in less than thirty minutes a crime committed, a police hunt for the suspect, the capture of the suspect, his trial and sentencing. In about an hour, a team of covered wagons will cross the breadth of the United States, engaging in pitched battles with bandits and Indians, trudging through blizzards and hundred-degree heat.

Commercials make the ordinary beautiful, the weak strong, and the dumb smart in as little as twenty seconds. In one minute, kids can see a child grow into a healthy youth by eating certain packaged bread. In thirty seconds they see a family's weekly supply of dirty clothes washed.

For the child, TV has accelerated his concept of time and movement between places and turned him into a creature who wants and expects instant responses to his wishes. On TV he sees people getting what they want immediately. If he sees this happening every day, he expects similar responses and action in real-life situations at home and in school. If he doesn't get it, he becomes frustrated and, in some instances, hostile.

7

Watching Mayhem
Hurts Children

The rate of violence is increasing in the United States. There is fear, anxiety, tension, anger, hostility, and desperation in the streets of America's cities. In places like New York it is not uncommon for people to have four or five locks with chains on their doors. More and more apartments are equipped with burglar alarms or German Shepherd dogs, sometimes both. Some people have even installed bars in their windows. Mugging has practically eliminated the nighttime stroll in the park. Car theft is up. So are assault, rape, and murder. The crime wave has swept into city schools. New York spent $6 million in 1972 to set up a small army of guards for its schools.[1] More rapes and muggings are reported on or near university campuses than ever before. Violence is spreading to suburbia, a place where former city dwellers fled to escape the urban murder and mugging.

"Today we are seeing more violence for the sake of violence," says clinical psychologist Israel Charney. "This is what we call random violence. It's the most frightening aspect of violence today because it's likely to

70

grow into epidemic proportions before we are able to deal with it."[2]

Youth are committing most of these acts of violence. Since 1963, juvenile delinquency has been increasing at a faster rate than the juvenile population.[3]

Sociologists and social psychologists probe for reasons for the increase in violence. Drug traffic, social frustration, self-hate, the heightening lust for material things, youth alienation toward our political and economic system, the breakup of the American family unit, hedonism made fashionable, and race hate are some of the reasons they give.

All of these reasons have causes, some so deep and complicated that skilled social psychologists cannot detect them. On the other hand, some are so obvious they are easily overlooked—television, for example. Of course the TV industry would pooh-pooh such a suggestion, asking in quick reflex: Prove it! True, there is no conclusive proof—not yet, but there is evidence, mounting evidence. In the meantime, while the industry offers a smug challenge to "prove it," there is a strong chance that what it is serving children on TV might be hurting them and teaching them antisocial behavior, making them ripe candidates for violent crime.

Common sense tells us television has to be a strong factor in the upward spurt of crime. Before the TV era, there was less crime. Our streets were safer; people did not think of barring their windows and doors; there was a greater trust among people. Now TV is everywhere, practically in every home. It is the medium people use most and trust most. Many of those who are twenty-five and younger were brought up with it and usually controlled the TV channel switcher before "Dad came home." They have feasted on a regular diet of shoot 'em ups, head-cracking, sword-fighting, whip-lashing and two-fisted tavern-brawling episodes. Superman, Hopalong Cassidy, Zoro, Tarzan, and Popeye were some of their heroes—men who were made to appear a notch above others, superior morally and physically—heroes who meted out justice with a blast from a six-shooter or a smash in the solar plexus.

"I didn't get my ideas from Mao, Lenin or Ho Chi Minh," cried a Yippie leader addressing a crowd of demonstrators and troops outside the Pentagon in 1968. "I got my ideas from the Lone Ranger."[4] That youth meant it. There must be many more youths who share the same feelings and who have never articulated them, but who express them by throwing rocks through windows.

We live in a violence-prone society. It has always been that way. The civilization white men carved out of the North American wilderness is based on the blood of the American Indian and the sweat of the black slave. During the frontier days the six-shooter was more sacred and powerful than the cross. We raped the land and destroyed the animal life on it. There were people—many of them—who applauded hangings, straining to see the trap door spring open. We honored our great warriors—Washington, Grant, Eisenhower—by making them president. We have assassinated presidents, too. We crave violence. Witness the mania over professional football—an activity of brutal body contact, or watch the bejeweled and the bedraggled together scream for "blood" at professional wrestling and boxing matches. The "might makes right" philosophical fiber runs prominently through the social fabric of our society.

The TV moguls know we are a violence-prone people, that we like to see a "good fight." So they have accommodated us with programs like *Mannix, Roadrunner, Bonanza, Gunsmoke,* and *Hawaii Five-O,* creating a monstrous situation in which our taste for violence is not only satisfied but reinforced.

It is an expensive taste, especially in terms of the behavior it teaches, the psychological damage it generates in our children. Day and night more than 100 million people watch more than 90 million sets in more than 68 million homes for more than seven hours. Into those homes TV unleashes hand-to-hand battlefield combat, murder, and verbal violence in the form of backbiting and character assault. A *Christian Science Monitor* survey in 1971 recorded in 74 hours of prime-time viewing one week, 217 incidents and threats of violence and 125 killings and murders.[5] The Barcus study found that about three of every ten dramatic segments in children's shows were saturated with violence and 71 percent had at least one instance of violence involving human beings. The study also showed that violence was presented in such a matter-of-fact way that children were led to believe violence was an acceptable means of self-expression.[6] By the age of fourteen the average American child has seen eighteen thousand killings on TV,[7] executed in a variety of ways—with hands, rocks, arrows, daggers, bullets, and bombs.

There has to be a link between televised violence and the brutality on our streets and the insensitivity many people show toward human suffering. Many TV-station general managers know television teaches and persuades viewers. If it did not, companies would not spend big money to advertise on stations. If commercials penetrate the consciousness of kids, and affect their behavior, isn't it reasonable to think that detective or cowboy and Indian episodes make a deep impression on them as well? The managers would like parents to believe that neither commercials nor program content affects their sons and daughters, that stabbing or tomahawking scenes make no dent on the consciousness of the child viewer. If they know in their hearts that television violence does affect the child's behavior and claim that it does not, then they are participating in an immoral act. If they are uncertain and still advocate airing shows like *Roadrunner* and *Popeye,* then they are cowards. If they simply do not know what the effects are and yet defend showing televised violence then they are ignorant and arrogant men.

TV violence impresses kids. Thousands of toy pistols, machine guns, bazookas, whips, daggers, and grenades have been sold because of television, and they are not put on shelves like trophies. They are used by kids in simulated shoot outs in backyards, alleys, parks, and streets, putting into practice what they have learned from TV westerns and war films. Some kids are so stimulated by what they see that stimulation erupts into reality. For example, a graduate student in psychology at Stony Brook University observed a youngster one day who had seen the program *Gigantor*—a program about battling robots—running around in the schoolyard hitting other children and screaming aloud, "I am Gigantor."[8]

That kind of incident is fairly common across our country. Kids see programs and try to execute what their heroes do. Sporadic exposure to video violence might not be harmful. But what about the millions of youngsters who every day get a dose of televised saloon brawls, frontier scalpings, and police and outlaw fire fights?

It is like water to a plant. Years pass and the seed of violence that was planted and continually nourished sprouts into an aggressive personality who discovers that the quickest solution to a conflict is a karate chop to the neck or a knee in the crotch, while others who are less physically endowed find the gun and knife doing the trick. These personalities, shaped to a great extent by televised violence, roam the street, their brains packed with such scenes as a Marine behind a machine gun repulsing the enemy, a commando knifing a sentry in order to blow up an enemy munitions plant, a cowboy carrying a kicking squaw into the woods. Their violence-potential level is greater than that of the kids of the forties and fifties, for they have had a life-long audiovisual education on the social merits of violence and how to execute it with sophistication. In the late 1960s youth who were brought up with TV assaulted the Justice Department, shook the gates of the Pentagon, rioted on university campuses, stole, raped, and murdered more than any other generation of youth, and the crime rate continues to spiral upward.

The sharp rise in violence in the sixties stunned the keepers of our government. Quickly, the National Commission on the Causes and Prevention of Violence was born, charged with finding the root causes of the jump in the amount of murder, assault, rape, and rioting in our society. In December 1969, the commission announced its findings. TV was mentioned: "Television enters powerfully into the learning process of children and teaches them a set of moral and social values about violence which are inconsistent with the standards of a civilized society."[9]

Despite the smokescreen set off by TV industry representatives on the Surgeon General's Committee concerning the results of its investigation into televised violence, a careful probe beneath the plethora of "howevers" in the final report reveals a clearer picture of the impact of TV violence on children.

Most of the scientists who participated in the Surgeon General's investigation revealed that their research clearly shows a link between televiewing and aggressive behavior. One massive study of children from eight to eighteen found a long-term correlation: the more chil-

dren watched violence on TV, the more socially aggressive they became.[10]

Another study sponsored by the Surgeon General con-
cluded that "violent fictional programs are seen by the
young as highly realistic, even more so than news and
documentaries."[11] In a four-week study conducted by
two Pennsylvania State University human-development
professors, one group of children was exposed to aggres-
sive-type programs like *Superman* and *Batman.* Another
group was shown programs like *Mister Rogers Neighborhood.* The professors observed that the day-to-day
behavior of the children who watched the "aggressive"
shows deteriorated noticeably while, in contrast, those
who watched the "pro-social" programs improved in
observing rules, tolerating delays, and persisting at daily
tasks.[12]

Dr. Robert Leibert, one of the scientists who served on
the Surgeon General's Committee, feels that a "steady
diet of televised gunfights, infantry attacks, and felony
arrests promotes aggressive behavior in a child."

He goes on to say that psychologists' "evidence supports the modeling theory of development—that what
you see guides what you do."[13] Children in the past
twenty-five years have seen lots of violence on TV,
especially on Saturday morning, when the largest kid
audience is assembled. Just how violent is Saturday
morning TV? Dr. George Gerbner, in a study done in
1971 for the Surgeon General's Committee, found: "It is
clear that children watching Saturday morning cartoons
had the least chance of escaping violence or of avoiding
the heaviest saturation of violence on all television."[14]

The University of Pennsylvania professor also found
that the "average cartoon hour had nearly six times the
violent rate of the average adult television drama
hour."[15]

Saturday morning is not the only period where violence is displayed on television. There's plenty of it on weekday mornings and afternoons after school hours. The prime-time evening fare has its share also. Even if the networks eliminated violence from their children's programming, televised violence would still exist. There are more than a thousand stations that are affiliated with networks but are not owned by them, and they run numerous syndicated kiddie shows—most of them cartoons packed with violence. Most of these shows are run during the weekday mornings and late afternoons.

The pressure on the networks to eliminate violence in children's programming is mounting. ACT's jabbing, adverse publicity, and some prodding from former FCC Chairman Dean Burch has moved ABC, CBS, and NBC to drop or clean up a few of their more violent Saturday morning shows. But the networks are still kicking and pressing their challenge for someone to prove conclusively that TV violence causes aggressive behavior in children. This, despite the fact the vice chairman of the Surgeon General's Committee, Dr. Eli Rubinstein, told a Senate committee in March 1972 that he is convinced of the causal relationship between violence on TV and antisocial behavior.[16] Surgeon General Jesse L. Steinfeld is also convinced. In fact, after the watered-down final report of the committee was released to the public, Steinfeld told *Newsweek* magazine, "If I had written this report alone, I would have written somewhat more strongly."[17]

Some scientists are running out of patience. They feel that immediate action has to be taken to curb violence on television. "We cannot wait for all of the evidence to come in," says University of California psychologist Percy Tannenbaum. "In this case it can never be all in. The real question is when do we as a society take action.

If there is a clear and present danger that televised violence is harmful to our children, then we should simply say, 'This is enough.' "[18]

There are some TV management people who believe video violence does not hurt a child. In fact, they claim, watching murder on television has a cathartic effect on children. It helps them release their hostilities through the TV characters with whom they identify.

Most psychologists, however, disagree with that theory. There is considerable evidence that supports the theory that observing violence, whether on TV or elsewhere, stimulates most people's aggressive nature. Furthermore, those who are stimulated and plunge into a fist fight and win have not released their aggressions. In fact, many psychologists contend, the victorious fight only reinforces the winner's aggressiveness. He has tasted triumph—and likes it and, remembering how his victory was achieved, is prone to strike again.[19] As for the loser, he just becomes more cautious as to whom he battles. He too would like to experience the feeling of conquest.

Televised violence cannot only make a child more physically aggressive, it can make him callous toward human suffering. For twenty-five years American children have witnessed cowboys shooting Indians and Indians scalping cowboys, soldiers mowing down the enemy with a machine gun, foolish hero clowns administering punishment by jabbing their thumbs in their associates' eyes or bouncing a hammer off their skulls. Day after day they watched this kind of mayhem, often while munching on popcorn and pretzels and sipping soda pop.

Psychologist Dan Anderson, who spent many hours before the TV set as a child, wonders if this exposure to televised crime and murder has affected his attitude toward violence and human suffering. An experience he had in the summer of 1972 made him think seriously about this question: "We were returning from Connecticut after an evening celebrating my wife's birthday with her parents. As we had done many times, we drove north into Massachusetts. We were warm, fed, comfortable, secure.

"The interstate highway was straight and wide—six lanes, three north, three south. We were in the middle lane going about seventy miles per hour. On our right a red Cadillac roared past us at a speed of about a hundred miles per hour. Within a few seconds a tan Ford went by at about the same speed. Their tail lights disappeared behind a slight rise.

"As we topped the rise we could see cars stopped in the road and people running. As I decelerated we heard five quick popping sounds and saw the Cadillac slowing around to go the wrong way on the highway. Quickly we were in the midst of the action: a uniformed policeman ran by on our left carrying a shotgun; a man in a sports jacket and tie leaped out of the Ford, drew a pistol and fired at the Cadillac. More shots were fired as we passed.

"We had just driven through a gunfight on a high speed road. Objectively, we were in substantial danger of our lives, yet we were not terribly excited, our hearts weren't rapidly beating, our palms weren't sweating, our knees weren't shaking. I've been more excited catching fish. Why? We'd seen the whole thing before, a thousand times before, on *Hawaii 5-0*, on the *Mod Squad*, on television.

"Our vicarious experience with TV violence completely inured us to real violence. Perhaps if we had seen blood or if a bullet crashed through our windshield we would have been upset. I don't know."

Quite a few youngsters derive sadistic pleasure from the murder and slaughter they experience on TV, an

instrument most preschoolers feel can do no wrong, can
bring no harm, is always right. How can something that
provides so much pleasure be harmful? they feel. So
they laugh when the cartoon character Roadrunner dies
nine times in six minutes; they laugh when the leader of
the Three Stooges twists the nose of one of his associates;
they laugh when Freddie Flintstone is knocked over by a
rolling boulder; they laugh when Deputy Dawg ties
knots in dogs' tails or swings a cat by its tail.

Television producers have a way of legitimizing laughter at acts of cruelty and violence. It is canned laughter.
Canned laughter reassures the child viewer that the
kicking of a cat or clubbing of a man is funny. After all,
kids reason, if everyone watching is laughing it must be
funny and okay to join in. So the idea that cruelty is funny
is reinforced in children every time canned laughter
follows a head-knocking or eye-poking scene, and they
grow up with a noticeable sadistic streak in them.

Thousands of youth laughed when rock singer Alice
Cooper glorified violence in a network TV special.
Cooper dismembered a doll while singing a sadistic song
and later pretended to hang himself. The youthful audience went wild, laughing and cheering.[20]

Scenes of one man clubbing another or a man jabbing a
knife into another man's heart are acts of violence people
are accustomed to seeing on TV. But there is another
form of violence on television that usually goes unno-
ticed—verbal violence, the nonphysical acts of violence,
which are exhibited on children's programming as well
as adult shows. There are scenes where hate is expressed
in a look and a barrage of ugly words, where cheating is
calculated and carried out, where human beings are
ridiculed, where backbiting and taking advantage of people's weaknesses are demonstrated and cynicism is expressed.

Kids learn from what they see on TV and believe that what they learn is sanctioned by their parents, for they reason: "If mom and dad allow me to watch TV, then everything I see on it must be acceptable, for they wouldn't allow me to see anything that would not be good for me." With that kind of "green light," a child adopts at least some of the nonphysical violent behavior portrayed realistically on the video tube as part of his behavior pattern. He learns how to con, to cheat, to break into sealed entrances. Pounding on a table to emphasize a point becomes a natural reflex in an argument, because one of his TV heroes does it.

There is a difference between protecting a child from televised violence and shutting him off from reality, keeping him from appreciating life as it is practiced all around him.

First, a parent must understand that preschoolers, even first, second, and third graders have difficulty distinguishing between reality and unreality. They tend to accept a lot of what they see on TV as real.

Most adults know that much of what is portrayed on television series and in movies is either exaggerated portrayals of living conditions or condensed real experiences. But young children are not that sophisticated. They embrace TV messages more readily. After all, they are purer, less complicated, take messages at face value, their minds are less cluttered than those of their parents. Because they are more open, more naive, they are more gullible and more susceptible to adopting what they see on TV as a part of their own behavior and outlook on life. The trouble is that a lot of what is considered realistic on TV is, in fact, not a true account of what life is really like either in the child-viewer's immediate environment—his neighborhood—or elsewhere. On most TV detective or western series there might be five fist fights and two gun battles in less than a half hour. That pace of violence simply doesn't exist in our society or any other society. Most children grow up never seeing a gun fight. Though crime is on the rise in the United States, it has not reached the intensity and fury portrayed on programs like *F.B.I.*, *Hawaii Five-0*, and *Mannix*.

No, keeping young children away from televised violence is not keeping them from reality, it is actually protecting them from becoming psychologically warped and overly aggressive; it could also protect them from flirting with crime.

Recognizing the need to keep children from watching televised violence is easier than actually preventing them from watching it, because behavioral habits, even in children, are difficult to break. Obviously, new parents have an advantage because they can start fresh to establish good TV viewing habits in their homes. The big problem is dealing with the child who truly enjoys watching Popeye heave his adversary over a ship or seeing a cowboy butt an Indian in the face with his rifle.

The biggest mistake parents make is in employing violence to prevent their children from watching programs like *Hawaii Five-0*. In other words, yanking a child away from the set and spanking him is only transferring into live action the kind of action parents do not want their children to see. Besides, in resorting to this kind of control, the parent puts the child on the receiving end of a violent act which can be physically and emotionally painful to him, possibly leaving deep psychological wounds, especially if the child has never been told why it was bad to watch violence on television.

In instituting controls, parents must first learn the depth of their child's attachment to violent programs, then try to understand what the attachment means to him.

Gaining such an understanding may take some effort on the part of the parent. Talking to a child about his favorite TV programs might provide the parent with some clues, but the parent must make certain the talk takes place away from the televiewing area. This, so the set doesn't become an obstacle to interpersonal communication. Perhaps the conversation could take place during a walk or at a picnic—in other words, on neutral ground during a fun time. The parent should wait until the child is relaxed and seems comfortable before introducing the TV-programming topic. The parent can help make the child comfortable by being in a placid state of mind during the meeting. This is important because a child responds more to the attitude of an adult than to his words. The idea is to become attuned to the child. And this is achieved by talking to the child with your mind and heart and will power as well as your voice.

Of course, the parent should avoid being blunt in approaching the subject. The idea is to have the child express freely his feelings about the violent programs he likes. Parents should never resort to interrogation. During the discussion, the parent should gently ask a question like, "Do you think Popeye is stronger than Superman?" This kind of question does not attack the child's hero, and if he feels comfortable, he will reveal some of his true feelings about why he likes Popeye. He might also reveal other sides of his personality that the parent did not know existed, all valuable information needed to wean him from TV violence.

But securing information is one thing, doing the right thing with it is a greater challenge. Dealing with the three-to-eleven-year-old child who has a deep attachment to violent programs or characters in those programs is perhaps the most strenuous undertaking in the weaning process. A harsh yanking away could turn the child against his parents. After all, the parent would be denying the child the source of perhaps his most precious pleasure. Substituting a non-TV interest for the child's TV interest could be the answer. But that interest has to be carefully selected. Since most children who like violent kinds of programs enjoy physical action, perhaps a good substitute would be involvement in a sport or outdoor game that requires some physical exertion. Finding an adequate substitute for televised violence would require an extra effort on the part of the parent. It might mean that a parent must sacrifice a personal pleasure in order to free his child from the clutches of video violence, a grip that could emotionally maim his child for life.

As for the child who has a mild fascination for the TV shoot 'em ups, there is no need to make elaborate plans to change his viewing habits. A simple explanation as to why such programming can be harmful would suffice, followed by a gentle but firm statement that he is not to watch televised violence until further notice. It should be put that way because the child should not be subject to an act of finality, made to feel that he was forbidden forever to watch certain kinds of programs. The parent should explain that when the child grows older, he'll be able to see programs he cannot watch now. In the explanation, the parent should point out to the child that the program prohibition is being instituted for his protection, that a great deal of televised violence could damage his emotional and social health. The parent should urge the child to trust him. The tone of the conversation is critical. The parent must be sympathetic—yet communicate certitude. It is important the child know his parent means what he is saying. On the other hand, it is also important for the parent to communicate to the child that he understands how he feels being deprived of watching certain programs.

In a household where there is a considerable age difference among children, weaning a young child away from violence in television could be a problem. After all, parents should not expect their teenagers to comply with the TV restrictions set for their preschool- or elementary-school-age brothers and sisters. They should be allowed greater TV freedom, for youth are usually better able to distinguish between reality and fantasy. But there are problems in a home with more than one child and only one TV set. The older children usually dominate the set and so the younger ones see what the older ones watch. The late popular child psychologist Haim Ginott in an article written for *Life* magazine in the fall of 1972, offered a way to handle this problem in his now famous scenario style: "One mother tried to cope with TV problems by saying to her fifteen-year-old son Jim: 'I have a problem and need your help. As you know, we have only one TV set. I'd rather that Craig (Jim's 8 year old brother) not watch tonight's special. It's too frightening. I know you want to watch it. Could you see it at your friend's home.'

"To Craig, who insisted on watching the program, the mother said: 'I wish this special were less violent and less scary, then I would feel comfortable about you watching it.' Craig: 'You mean I can't watch it?' Mother: 'It's too violent.' Craig: 'How come Jim can?' Mother: 'You tell me.' Craig: 'I don't know.' Mother: 'I'm sure you are able to figure it out.' Craig: 'Cause he's older.' Mother: 'You figured it out.' Craig: 'But I still want to watch it.' Mother: 'I know you are disappointed and wish you were older!' Craig: 'Yeah.' However more he complains, the mother can say, 'I know.' "[21]

Persuading commercial television to eliminate televised violence from its programming will not be easy. After all, the stations operate to make a profit, and they seem to be prospering by employing their present programming pattern.

For TV stations, bigger audiences mean bigger profits. To build big audiences, they feel, shows must capture the attention of the viewer, and a punch in the face or a gun duel at high noon has proven to be a reliable audience magnet.

There is evidence, however, that children's programming need not contain violence to be popular. *Sesame Street, Mr. Rogers Neighborhood* and the *Electric Company* are good examples. The audiences they pull would certainly attract eager and wealthy advertisers.

The way has been shown to create popular nonviolent children's programs. Now the commercial television people must take the courageous step to alter their programming pattern for children.

If and when they take that step they should take to heart the suggestion of Yale University Medical College Professor Richard H. Granger: "In medicine a basic principle is 'First, do no harm.' It seems that television might well adopt this as its first principle for children's programming. If so, it might meet that goal by insisting that those creative people who devise and produce programs for children become thoroughly familiar with the knowledge which already exists about child growth and development."[22]

8

TV Turns Children
into Racists

Little Larry likes TV, especially cartoons and adventure shows. He enjoys watching cowboys beat Indians in fights and outnumbered white men defeat legions of spear-carrying African natives. He distrusts any olive-skinned, black-haired humans with almond-shaped eyes.

Larry is only five, yet he has been infected by racism, a social disease he has no concept of. He has never met Indians, Africans, or orientals face to face. His only encounter with them has been through television. TV played a major role in infecting Larry and thousands of other white children in the United States.

Larry's infection is not part of a TV station or network plot. It is just that racism has been deeply woven into the social fabric of the American life and TV is a part of that way of life. Its producers—many of whom are progressive-minded—are unaware of their racism. They are unaware, because racism is a subconscious feeling of superiority. It is a social disease that most white American adults have inherited and carry with them, exposing it in their relations with their families, in their play and their work. The people who produced the *Porky Pig* cartoon that depicts the Indian as a bloodthirsty savage are basically good people who have no desire to hurt anyone, but they don't truly equate the American Indian with the white man even though they may claim they do. Racism cannot be wiped away by reading books, though that might be a step toward eliminating it. It requires a change of heart.

The people who put together the Raid insect remover commercial that depicts pesty insects as slanty-eyed, sneaky orientals are probably people who don't consider themselves racists. Yet, they did not choose a white figure to portray the villain. They dug into their bag of stereotypes and selected the kind of human being most people in the United States could identify as shady and dangerous, someone who could hurt you. In the older people, this kind of TV message revives the World War II slogan "The only good Jap is a dead one." As for the children—they begin to associate evil with orientals and the infection begins to fester.

Kids sit before the TV set, unconscious candidates for racism. They are unaware of what's happening to them, and the people who are designing racist programs are unaware of the kind of poison they are creating and transmitting.

Often TV series writers are unconscious of the racism that spews from their pens. In fact, some of what they consider to be their funniest lines are humiliating thousands of viewers of a certain race or nationality and reinforcing deep-seated predjudices in millions of others. For example, on the program *M-A-S-H*, on December 10, 1972, orientals were slurred. The setting was an army tent occupied by the show's major character. Lying on his bed was a wounded North Korean soldier. In trying to assure the prisoner that he was going to be treated well, Captain Pierce (the major character) ordered his South Korean interpreter to tell the North Korean, "We don't want to treat him like a wounded egg roll." Millions of nonorientals probably laughed at that line without ever considering the ache, the anger that it must have triggered in Korean-American and Chinese-American viewers.

A lot of laughs were registered at the expense of the Puerto Ricans on the January 1, 1973, *New Bill Cosby Show*. Bill Cosby, who won acclaim for his efforts in the Xerox series on the plight of the American black, and singer Pearl Bailey were involved in a short skit. Pearl Bailey, playing the role of a seductress, was alone with Bill Cosby in what was supposed to be his home. She tells him that his wife has gone shopping and then proceeds to tell him, "I checked her closet and she has more pointed shoes than the Puerto Rican army."

Even in newscasts, which are supposed to strive for objectivity and be free of bias, racism raises its ugly head. Robert Cirino in his book *Don't Blame the People* cites a number of examples of television journalism racism. Here is one: "Huntley-Brinkley had a 3:10 minute filmed report on Rhodesia near election time in June 1969. The report was a very favorable portrayal in film of a wealthy white businessman, his home, his wife and children, and business. NBC's dialogue was also favorable, characterizing the businessman as 'hardworking, fast moving, technical and western.' The NBC reporter noted that the businessman had little in common with the 'underdeveloped' and 'primitive,' black Rhodesian. Two-thirds of the report focused exclusively on the businessman and his family and included a forty-five-second interview in which the businessman and his wife expressed their political and segregationist viewpoints from the patio of their luxurious home. A portion of the report was devoted to describing the situations of the businessman's black employees, but not one of them was interviewed as to his viewpoints on politics or the racial situation. In all, the entire report and especially the unbalanced interviewing would have won a stamp of approval from the whites of Rhodesia—but not from the blacks. During the next two and one half months during which Huntley-Brinkley was monitored, there were no reports to counter this bias."[1]

A common manifestation of racism on TV which appears frequently and very innocently and is rarely caught by most white people is the dress of the villain and the good guy in most kiddie adventure shows. Invariably, the evil one is dressed in black and the hero is dressed in white. Symbolically, black is made to be bad, ugly, and wrong, and white is pure, good, and righteous. The child TV viewer, exposed to this kind of symbolism almost every day, internalizes it and employs it as part of his judgment mechanism of people.

Almost every day television reinforces racism in most white middle-class viewers, unbeknownst to them and the people who produce the programs. But there are people watching who are hurt by it. Black, Chicano, Puerto Rican, Indian, Oriental Americans receive a regular dose of racism. It gnaws away at their self-image; it deepens their feelings of inferiority; it fuels their hostility toward the white man and his white-oriented society; it is a divisive force in a country where a lot has been said about the need to unite the American people. But what makes racism on TV so difficult to stamp out is its invisibility in most white homes and governmental councils. How can you combat something you cannot recognize?

Even programs that are considered good children's fare, that are designed to convey healthy moral messages, unwittingly reinforce racism. One pathetic example of this occurred on February 20, 1973, on an ABC network program called *Super Star Movie,* which featured a Lassie episode. It was pathetic because the producers obviously tried to show how American Indians are often treated unjustly. Though they accomplished their objective, they also did a splendid job of extolling the virtues of the "White Man's Burden."

The movie was about a sleezy white businessman who cons the people on an Indian reservation to give up a lot of their land so that he can establish a resort in which they would be part owners. When the Indian people discover the white businessman's true intentions, they become angry and threaten violence. At this point, Lassie's family, very middle-class white, step into the situation and are able to extinguish the fire in the hearts of the Indians, calming them down. In a very patronizing way, they show the Indians where to go to bring the white business swindler to justice.

The whole episode was simply another case of the whites knowing more than nonwhites, of whites being a superior people having a manifest responsibility to guide the weaker races. White children see this and internalize it.

"Seeing is believing," says Boston University psychology professor Ralph Gary. Professor Gary warns that children's belief in the truth of television "can lead to startling misconceptions. . . . Inevitably, misconceptions, whatever their source must stand the test of experience and be corrected. Where they do not, they become a base for preconceptions and prejudice!"[2]

For twenty-five years, the minorities in the United States have watched TV, and not only have they seen their races run down, sometimes overtly and other times subtly, but they have seen a world which they find difficult to identify with: Fair-skinned, blond, and blue-eyed parents going to church made up of the same kind of people, living in neighborhoods where darker-skinned people never appear. Most minority children who watched TV regularly during the past two decades, lived in two worlds: the world of their home and family, and the world of television. The black, Chicano, Puerto Rican, and Indian kids compared the two worlds—a painful process that attacks their self-esteem and feeds their anger.

From 1947 to 1967, *Amos and Andy, Beulah* and the *Little Rascals* were the only TV shows in which black characters were central figures. Beulah was a maid who seemed to typify the slave era in-house mammie, someone with earthly wisdom, but who could never rise socially above the station of a server of elegant suppers. The characters in *Amos and Andy* were made to appear irresponsible, shiftless, and immoral. Only pressure from the NAACP and other civil-rights groups forced the show off the air in 1963. As for the two little blacks on the *Little Rascals,* they were simply play objects for the other kids who were all white. Their eye popping and eye rolling and speedy running away from frightening situations were stereotype characterizations of alleged black behavior.

The black child rarely saw any healthy models he could look up to, anyone he could realistically relate to. In 1966 a television study conducted by UCLA revealed that blacks were given only 0.65 percent of the speaking roles in commercials and 1.39 percent of the nonspeaking roles. Blacks fared somewhat better in the program portion, with a 3.36 percent of the speaking roles and 8.49 percent of the nonspeaking roles.[3]

There has been some improvement, but not much. Most of the progress has been made in the adult programming sector. There are the *Bill Cosby* and *Flip Wilson* shows and Lloyd Haynes in *Room 222.* And there are a few more black faces in a number of adventure series and commercials. But the situation is still poor in the children's programming sector.

A pilot study commissioned by ACT found that non-American and nonwhite cultures were referred to negatively almost every time they were mentioned and that black and other minority characters made up only a small percentage of characters—7 percent black and 2 percent other minorities.

The study carried out by Black Efforts for Soul in Television examined fourteen half-hours of Saturday children's television programs. All figures of authority or sources of information were white and all four references to American Indians were derogatory.

William Wright, the director of the organization that did the study, told the symposium on Children and Television at Yale University in the fall of 1972, "It is horrifying to realize how much stereotyped thinking and bigoted information is being absorbed by young minds watching these [Saturday children's] programs."[4]

9

TV Perpetuates
Female Inferiority Myth

Television pretty much reflects the prevailing mood and thinking of the nation. If a foreign woman watches it, she could gain a fairly accurate picture of the interests, concerns, and problems of most Americans. She could also secure an understanding of the social condition of the country. One thing she'll notice, especially if she comes from a country where the equality of the sexes flourishes, is how deeply rooted male chauvinism is in the United States. She'll notice it, because TV reinforces it.

Like racism, sexism is a subconscious feeling of superiority. The male producers, directors, and writers putting together television shows don't consider themselves women haters. But they do believe that women should know "their place." And that place is usually behind the sink, in an office taking shorthand, or in a hospital picking up bedpans. In the American way of life, the woman is treated as "the weaker sex." What does this mean to most men? It means a woman isn't as bright as a man, isn't as strong as a man, and needs to be cared for by a man. And though he never says so, he acts as if a woman's primary role in life is to be a major source of his pleasure.

In most of the programs that children watch, there rarely is a female who is the major decision maker, who is the strongest, the brightest, and most stable character. The woman is usually portrayed as someone who needs direction from a man, someone who is not too depend-able and cannot make a decision and often someone who is a bit scatterbrained.

When a woman is the leading character of a show she is usually portrayed as someone who succeeds in gaining her objectives by cunning and manipulation. The *Lucy* show is a case in point, especially the early series which today are being shown as reruns either in the morning or the afternoon in many communities. In them, Lucy is constantly shown plotting to arrange for matters to go her way, usually at the expense of unsuspecting males. Shows like that reinforce the myth that women are foxy by nature and cannot be trusted. It also teaches little girls that when they grow up they will have to act the same way as Lucy to succeed in life.

In a study which analyzed the sex roles presented on children's TV programs, Dr. Sarah Sternglands and Dr. Lisa Serbin of the State University of New York at Stony Brook found:

—There were twice as many males on children's TV programs as females.

—Males were overwhelmingly more aggressive than females. They did all of the punching, belittling, name calling, and murdering.

—Males appeared wiser than females and were the ones who almost always provided comfort and sym-pathy to the lost one or the weak one.

—Females were the people who sought aid. They were made out to be dependent ("the weaker sex").

—Males were far more likely to be rewarded for an activity than a female.

—When females were successful in some activity, it wasn't because of their knowledge, strength, or special human skill. It was because they used magic.

—Females were more likely to be ignored. If they proposed a course of action, it was usually brushed aside by a male character.[1]

Most commercials reinforce sexism. The cosmetic ads urge women to beautify themselves so they can better please their man, so they can be a more effective sex slave. The bath bead ads which stress female softness are a good example of that. There is a mini-cigar commercial that makes women appear shallow and dumb, demonstrating that all it takes to lure them into a man's love nest is a glimpse and whiff of his mini-cigar. Another commercial makes viewers believe that all a woman is good for is scrubbing "the ring out of her husband's collar." If she will drink a certain tonic that is heavily endowed with iron, one commercial tells the woman viewer, she will be a more energetic house cleaner, cook, baby-sitter, and bed mate. Again, the stereotype role of a woman is reinforced.

True, there is some effort on TV to elevate the status of women in our society, but much of that effort is directed to the adult sector of TV programming. Some attempts to promote the cause of woman's liberation have been fairly successful in *All in the Family, Marcus Welby,* and the *Mary Tyler Moore Show.* But that contribution is like trying to light up the night with a match. Besides, what good a few series episodes accomplish is undermined by the frequent sly digs and sarcasm of male comedians whenever the feminist struggle is mentioned.

By watching the present television program and commercial fare, little girls are being brainwashed about what their role will be in the future as an adult. They are made to believe that when they grow up they are expected to be essentially a baby factory. Witness all of the doll commercials on Saturday morning television, dolls that not only cry but wet their pants, can be fed, walk and talk and sing rock n' roll songs and seem to have more and more of the characteristics of a real baby.

Today's female preschooler is taught that her professional choices are more limited than a boy's. TV primes her to become a secretary, nurse, teacher, and, if she is tough enough, a factory assembly worker or saleslady. Boys are not immune to TV's sexism. They learn rather quickly that the man is the boss in our society. After all, there is no female Superman, Lone Ranger, Batman, Underdog, or female journalist reporting from battlefields in Vietnam or the Middle East. TV conditions them to be sexists like the males of past generations and, tragically, without their understanding what sexism is.

10

The Unauthorized
Sex Educator

It is 3:30 P.M. in the Springfield, Massachusetts, area. Seven-year-old Mary and nine-year-old Stanley race into the house, dash to the TV room, and turn on the set. No spinach-swallowing Popeye or soaring Mighty Mouse is on the screen. Something in real human flesh is capturing their interest—the kissing, embracing, and seducing on *One Life to Live.* Following that soap opera, the youngsters are treated to a carefully constructed lesson on the art and science of sexual seduction from the program *Love American Style.* Thirty minutes later they switch channels and watch Merv Griffin talk about sex with a group of so-called experts in the field. During the discussion, actress Zsa Zsa Gabor unveils some titillating tidbits about her love affairs. While orchestrating the discussion, Merv Griffin is busy squeezing every juicy detail out of her. Zsa Zsa also offers an opinion of nudity which really has no sociological significance, but does heighten the show's sexuality.

Unfortunately, many children like Mary and Stanley across the United States are exposed to such TV fare. These children usually have complete television viewing freedom and have parents who are either ignorant of TV's power to teach or who are simply uninterested in interfering with their children's television viewing habits or altering their TV tastes.

Now, if parents show no concern, should the TV industry and government care? They should, and for the same reason the government should protect us from pollution. True, so far, men and women are not stripping naked on TV as they are on films shown in theaters, but they do come close. Besides, a facial expression, a sigh, a groan, a bump and grind can communicate more sexuality than an exposed bosom.

True, talk shows like Merv Griffin that are aired in the afternoon are directed at the housewife. However, the time they are shown in many areas is considered the peak kid-watching period during the weekday. In the home where the noise of playing kids is not tolerated, where TV is used as an anesthetizer, children usually control the TV set and could easily develop a liking for programs like *Love American Style,* and no one is going to stop them from watching that kind of show.

The TV industry used to consider Sunday 8 P.M. as a family TV-watching hour. For many years during that time families watched the *Ed Sullivan Show.* Ed's sign-off was considered a signal for children to go to bed on Sundays. But when families tune in CBS at 8 P.M. on Sunday in the 1972-73 TV season they were exposed to *M-A-S-H,* a program centered around a cluster of sex-starved soldier doctors and nurses based at a war front hospital. Sex seems to be every character's preoccupation. The November 5, 1972, episode, for example, showed an army psychiatrist dressed in his underwear trying to seduce a nurse clad only in a slip. The tussle ends up in the nurse's bed with the psychiatrist embracing the young lady known as "Hot Lips." Quite a departure from the Hungarian trapeze artists and talking-dog acts that would appear on Ed Sullivan's show. The trouble is that though programs change on TV, the family TV-watching pattern remains the same: 8 P.M. Sunday still remains a family TV-watching time, despite Ed Sullivan's departure from that time slot, and television programming executives know it.

I am not advocating the elimination of programs like *M-A-S-H*, *Love American Style*, or the *Merv Griffin Show*, only that their availablility to the child viewer should be eliminated. Considerable pressure should be placed on TV-network management and TV-station operators to reorganize their program scheduling so that children don't have an opportunity to see programs like *Love American Style* or talk shows like *Mike Douglas, Johnny Carson*, or *Merv Griffin*. As for soap operas, they should be aired when children are asleep. There are entirely too many preschoolers who get a daily dose of young ladies combating nymphomania, wives and husbands committing adultery, and teenagers giving birth out of wedlock—all from watching soap operas. These messages emanating from sex-oriented daytime shows do not bounce off the little skulls of three, four, five-year-olds and the elementary school children who watch television after school. They are absorbed.

Some of my university students who have observed children watching TV have confirmed that this process takes place. They have noticed youngsters expressing interest and some understanding of soap-opera themes.

One student reported that she observed a five-year-old insist on seeing *Love Is a Many Splendored Thing* instead of *Sesame Street*. The child claimed she watched the soap opera regularly with her mother. The little girl got her way. "I was really amazed," reported the student, "that she could tell me exactly what had happened and what it all meant. It really showed me that these children really do understand those programs that adults so glibly say will be over their heads."

Another student filed this report on a five-year-old boy she observed watching TV: "At 4:30 he had the choice of *Love American Style, I Love Lucy* or *Flintstones*. He chose *Love American Style*. The show had three parts. The first concerned a couple divorcing, the second, wife swapping, and the third, a wedding night. Of all the programs he watched that afternoon he seemed to enjoy *Love American Style* the most. He giggled and curled up in the chair. He seemed to accept the plots without question. When I asked him if he understood the meaning of divorce and wife swapping, he answered that of course he did, that he wasn't a boy any more."

Even if sex-oriented shows were programmed for the hours when children are in bed, kids will still be exposed to commercials which emphasize sex seduction more often and more effectively than most programs.

"Commercials," Ben Bagdikian writes in *The Information Machines*, "uses sexuality in ways that are forbidden on the stage, in schools, and in the nonadvertising parts of television, but that are accepted because they are commercial."[1] Many children, especially preschoolers, enjoy commercials more than programs, because their messages are simple, are delivered in a lively, stimulating manner in a very short span of time, no more than a minute. Imagine, a seven, eight, nine, ten, or eleven-year-old, more sophisticated than a preschooler, watching a bikini-clad, voluptuous young lady saunter sexily toward a he-man type lighting up a mini-cigar. When they meet, he passes her a thin, brown capsule of tobacco; in the close-up shot, she takes a drag, her face rapt in passionate ecstasy. Seconds later, the couple, their arms locked around each other's waists, leave their rendezvous point on the beach for a private place to do what comes naturally for happily married couples, except that this couple have apparently just met.

There are scores of commercials that are equally lewd. Hair tonic, mouthwash, shaving cream, cigars, pipe tobacco, shampoos, after-shave lotions, mattresses, brassieres, panty hose, vitamins, and so-called health tonics are sold on TV as the promised sex elixir, empowered to provide the user with incomparable, irresistible sexual charm. The episodes created to sell these products are put together by some of the world's best communicators who are supported by psychologists, expert in breaking through human defenses and arousing human passion.

Even a conscientious parent has no sure-proof way of guarding his children from this "stag movie" onslaught, for the sex-oriented commercials pop up during the normal TV viewing hours for children. There is nothing to warn the parent that a sex-seducing kind of commercial will appear during a specific program or time. This has proven to be embarrassing to parents and children alike, when watching TV together. It has happened to our family. For example, one time while watching what was billed as a wholesome program, a commercial selling pre-electric-shave lotion popped up, featuring a young couple necking in a theater; the girl smells his lotion, becomes deeply aroused, runs her hands through his hair, caresses him, squeezes him, and whispers in a sultry voice, "Hold me barber close." Another time while I was watching the *Today* show, an excellent public-affairs program, with my eleven and twelve-year-old sons, the local TV station's news insert, sponsored by a mattress company, came on. Before the news was delivered, a one-minute commercial selling mattresses was shown. It was good enough to make someone's stag movie repertoire. A shapely young lady—actually, a well-known sex pot—dressed in a sheer negligee does a sexy running dance on a beach. When she makes it to a mattress lying on the sand, she dances around it and lays her shapely figure on it and proceeds to caress it, all the while, singing about how lovely it is, how enjoyable it is to sleep on. "Should I turn it off?" I wondered. "But if I do that, what would my boys think?" I left it on, rationalizing, "A minute of burlesque couldn't hurt them." Unfortunately, there have been many more provocative one-minute sequences they have been exposed to. What scares me is, when you add up all those minutes, what has all of that sexual stimulation on TV done to my children and the millions of other children in our country?

If no one knows the answer, should we gamble with our children, allowing them to be exposed to sex-oriented TV ads? I don't think so. Perhaps the networks and local TV stations could help by preparing and publishing a list of all commercials to be aired, rating them the way the movie industry does its films. If they refuse to do this, perhaps they could be pressured by the Federal Communications Commission or organizations like Action for Children's Television to air "sexy" commercials only in the evening when children are asleep.

The industry shows no sign of cleaning up the airwaves. In fact, the reverse seems to be happening.

The TV fare in 1972 and 1973 was more open, more sexually daring, than that of the year before. Even *TV Guide* (October 14, 1972) noticed this trend: "Startled [TV] viewers have seen explicitly sexy movies such as *A Man and a Woman*, *The Anderson Tapes*, and *The Damned*. Full frontal nudity has turned up on stations of the Public Broadcasting System and seems no more than a year or two away in commercial programming. Topics such as lesbianism are freely discussed on talk shows, while comedy shows feature humor that a 1966 audience would have considered improper outside a stag party. Daytime soap operas deal frankly with adultery and even show unmarried couples in bed together."

Certainly, the advertisers and their agencies who have considerable sway with TV management don't show any signs of de-emphasizing sex in their ads these days. In fact, they are producing sexually bolder ads. *Newsweek* (April 16, 1973) spotted this trend: "Sex has been used as an advertising come-on for years. But the ad writers always held back—the sexual message was more suggestive than explicit. No more. In advertisement after advertisement these days, the sexy sell is bold and brassy. . . . Ads directed at women, which at one time only hinted at a man's presence, now show mates in tawny, muscled glory—usually in the bedroom.

'What's going on? Some Madison Avenue theorists trace the sexy sell to the permissive society. . . ."

Several useful addresses:

Federal Communications Commission
1919 M Street, N.W.
Washington, D.C. 20580

Federal Trade Commission
Bureau of Consumer Protection
Washington, D.C. 20580

Action for Children's Television
46 Austin Street
Newtonville, Massachusetts 02160

American Broadcasting Company
1330 Avenue of the Americas
New York, N.Y. 10019

Columbia Broadcasting System
51 West 52nd Street
New York, N.Y. 10019

National Broadcasting Company
30 Rockefeller Plaza
New York, N.Y. 10020

Public Broadcasting Service
955 1'Enfant Plaza, S.W.
Washington, D.C. 20024

The addresses of your local television stations are listed in the phone book. Letters of complaint should be addressed to the station's general manager.

11

The Materialist-Maker Machine

Marty's presence before the TV set on Saturday mornings is as certain as the sunrise. In his home, as in many other homes, kids watching TV are more acceptable than kids playing in the house, for during the weekend parents like to sleep later and television keeps kids quiet. But this kind of permissiveness is costly and usually backfires. One place where backfiring occurs is in the supermarket.

On Saturday morning Marty is huckstered by cereal companies, sneaker firms, soda pop producers, candy makers, bicycle manufacturers, and a dozen other product producers. The boy doesn't have to wait a week to see these products again, and advertisers and their agencies know this. Marty unwittingly becomes an uncommissioned, unpaid salesman for the advertisers.

While being wheeled down the aisle in a supermarket cart, Marty spots a cereal he wants.

"Mommy," he cries, "get Sugar Nut Squares! It has a big whistle."

When Marty's mother refuses to purchase the cereal,

the boy screams. Embarrassed, she picks the box off the shelf and throws it into the cart. A smile flashes across Marty's tear-stained face. But it is a false victory for Marty, for nutritionally the cereal is practically worthless and the prize whistle breaks after five blows. But more seriously, the boy's spirit has been assaulted; Marty has been seduced into becoming a materialist without really understanding what materialism is.

Unfortunately, what is happening to Marty is happening to millions of kids like Marty all over our country.

Commercials nourish children's appetites for things. So do many programs children watch. TV teaches young children that the most meaningful rewards in life are whistles found in cereal boxes, walking and talking child-size dolls with a complete wardrobe of clothes, ten-speed bikes, new big cars, vacations at luxury hotels on a tropical isle or on a snow-covered mountain top. A quick review of TV's game shows, soap operas, commercial children's TV programs, and prime-time fare will substantiate what I am pointing out.

Some psychiatrists and childhood specialists have noticed television's materialistic brainwashing process taking its toll of children and parents. Dr. Theodore I. Rubin, a psychiatrist and columnist for the *Ladies Home Journal*, wrote in the January 1972 issue: "Television promotes the belief that a person will be socially rejected unless he or she owns certain material things. This is particularly worrisome when children are made to believe they must have a special toy to achieve happiness. Aside from the way this materialism distorts values, it also makes parents who can't afford those toys feel guilty."

The religious family as well as the irreligious family is affected by the materialism on TV. Television has penetrated the defenses of churches and synagogues against

TV's materialistic messages. For the most part, TV has more sway with a child than a minister, priest, or rabbi. This is mainly because most children have more experience with TV than with a clergyman; also, the experience with TV has been enjoyable and nonthreatening, which is not always the case in a child-clergyman encounter.

In a sense, materialism is being proselytized like a religion over TV—and with evangelical fervor. Advertised products are supposed to provide a viewer with all of the feelings and beliefs religion is supposed to provide: an inner strength to meet the problems of life, happiness and joy, a feeling of security, a loving, kind, and positive personality, even faith and purpose in life. Purchasing a certain car, for example, provides a person "with something to believe in"; drinking a particular brand of coffee "is heavenly."

Materialistic values are inculcated in most viewers through TV. These values are taught by the behavior that's on the tube.

A value that TV teaches well is exploitation. In fact, the exploiter is glorified on TV. How is this done? TV gives status to the character who takes advantage of people's weaknesses. There are plenty of examples of this kind of behavior, especially in children's cartoons. Bugs Bunny, for example, is continually making most of the creatures around him look like buffoons. He thrives on their ignorance and awkwardness.

Greed is another value that TV teaches effectively. In quiz games like *Let's Make a Deal,* contestants are continually trying to outbid the other guy. The shrewdest bargainer emerges as the winner—the hero.

Winning at all cost is a value that is stressed. So is self-centeredness, sensuality, and superficiality. These values are taught on commercials as well as in programs.

Tragically, most viewers are not aware that this teaching process is taking place. For most people still view TV as an entertainment vehicle provided for them free by advertisers. They believe they are free agents, able to choose the programs that interest them most. However, they fail to realize that in what they consider to be their tastes and preferences they have been conditioned by TV.

Ours is a materialistic society, despite what is said and written by some professional religionists in seminaries, monasteries, and parish-house libraries, and despite the passionate rhetoric of the revolutionaries who engineered the break of the American colonies with the British Crown. Television per se is not solely to blame for molding our children into materialists. It is only one tool—granted, a powerful one—in the materialist-making process in our country. Television describes and reflects quite accurately our material needs, our material desires, even our silent gnawing ones. Materialism was here long before TV. Television only helps to expand its influence, tighten its grip on the American soul.

We find ourselves caught in a sinister cycle where materialist writers and producers shape materialistically oriented programs which TV transmits to materialistic audiences that approve of the programs and clamor for more of the same and get it.

But there are some Americans, most of them youth, who have noticed the cycle and have withdrawn from it. And commercial television inadvertently has played a role in freeing them from the cycle's whirl. Their dropping out seemed to begin in the mid-1960s.

When you consider the statistic that the average eighteen-year-old American has already been exposed to 350,000 TV commercials,[1] you can understand why some kids go streaking to the hills. Imagine all of the beer, cereal, mouthwash, candy, girdle, toothpaste, panty hose, mattress, soda pop, potato chip, pretzel, hot dog, cat food, automobile, razor blade, wine, dog food, toy, and bologna images and sounds that have bombarded a growing teenager's brain since his first encounter with TV. For some youth, the exposure and absorption of such an avalanche of consumer items has set off a psychic regurgitation. They literally and figuratively want to purge themselves of all accumulated and inherited things, concepts, and mores that smack of a social order that they feel is obsessed with materialism. Some among them have even severed all ties with their parents, who they feel are contaminated by materialism. They curse phoniness and yearn for naturalness. They have an aversion to luxury and the processes that lead toward the acquisition of it. They bristle at the sight or mention of the trappings and social rituals of modern America. They seek freshness, new ways; they desire to climb spiritual heights, welcoming such struggles as a means to true emancipation. Sometimes, tragically, their search plunges them into a period of horror. In their probing, they take a wrong turn which psychologically maims them for life.

A great many youth today, however, have adopted the precepts of materialism, thanks to TV's superb job of brainwashing. Unlike their parents, whose materialism was born out of the daily struggle to find enough food to eat during the great depression in the 1930s, many of these young people, especially those from the middle class, want things and objects without struggling for them. It is as if what they see and like on TV, they believe is theirs or should be theirs. And their parents usually get them what they demand, sometimes reluctantly because something inside them is aware of the consequences of spoiling a child. But parents usually bow to the demand because they don't quite understand what makes today's high-school and college-age people tick, and they are obsessed with maintaining household tranquility. In reality, they don't really know children, and they find themselves in the pitiful position of buying their love and respect.

There's a lot more that upsets them. They worry about their children's lack of initiative and volition, of their disdain for working for what they want. They're puzzled and hurt, for they don't know why their children grew up the way they did.

The tragedy is that they must bear most of the blame, though they did nothing malicious. In fact, they worked hard to create a comfortable home, a house with two garages, a carefully manicured lawn, membership at the country club, and a cleaning woman. They bought their children the best clothes and toys and took them to the best hotels during the family vacation time.

But it was what they didn't do that contributed to the kind of outlook their children have as they approach adulthood. One of their most grievous errors of omission was to have forfeited much of their parental responsibility to the "third parent" in their home, television. TV comforted the kids when they were lonely and brought them hours and hours of pleasure, making them susceptible to TV's demands to do its bidding. The children were turned into consumers, expecting their demands to be answered as fast as they switched channels. TV has made them into materialists—like their parents, except that their philosophical interpretation and style is different.

Dr. Daniel C. Jordan, the director of the Center for the Study of Human Potential at the University of Massachusetts School of Education (in a personal communication on April 19, 1973), feels the materialistic thrust of television is derailing many children from knowing their true

selves: "What we become depends almost entirely on
what we learn and what we learn is for the most part
limited to the experiences we have. Among the most
critical aspects of any experience are all of the cues that
define the nature of man—all of the bits and pieces of
information, whether factual or emotional in nature, that
tell us who we are. Since television figures prominently
in the experience of children, it is important to examine
the kinds of views coming from television programming
that speak to our own natures. I suspect that the most
fundamentally damaging view of man that is perpetually
emphasized on television is that he is a material being
rather than a spiritual one. To know and to love are two
basic capacities of man that enable him to transcend the
limitations of materiality. If a human being cannot love or
does not know how to be loved, he may withdraw entirely
and become more like a vegetable or he may strike out
and become worse than a beast. To be loved, one must be
lovable and to be lovable means to acquire virtues, such
as kindness, courtesy, fairness, helpfulness, hopefulness,
and compassion. Yet, the thesis presented by television is
that having love is indeed desirable and you can get it by
using the right cosmetics, the right hair sprays, the best
deodorants, certain clothes, particular foundation gar-
ments; use the right toothpaste and mouth washes, chew
a particular gum, smoke the right cigarettes, serve the
appropriate beer, wash your clothes with the most powerful detergents, ad infinitum, and you will become lovable
and will therefore be loved. Love is thus made dependent upon commercially available material things. It is
difficult to imagine a greater distortion of a truth so basic
to our sanity. Love comes to us through the spiritualiza-
tion of our characters and through no other means.

"Even the plots of the dramatic serials focus on the
material aspect of our lives and do not deal with fun-

damental issues in a way that orients us to basic realities. For instance, a fair percentage of movies and serialized programs center around violence and exalt the capacity for 'steel nerves,' in fighting crime or perpetrating it. There is little emphasis on the means by which moral virtues are acquired and a positive emphasis placed upon the struggle to acquire them. The criminal appears as given and after several violent episodes, he is apprehended or killed and the drama ends. Again, the superficial events in the lives of people are portrayed and not the deep underlying needs and meanings. We know that human beings who are not loved and who experience repeated rejection are likely to become criminals or mentally ill or both. To experience love, one must attract it and this depends upon a spiritual force and not material ones."

12

An Irresistible Salesman, a Dollar Bonanza

Advertisers spend about $3 billion a year in television, financing the production of forty-three thousand commercials.[1] Common sense tells us that if the commercials weren't motivating viewers to purchase the products they were pushing—and that certainly is influencing human behavior—advertisers wouldn't invest so heavily in TV. There are advertisers that vie for the opportunity to spend $100,000 for one minute on television, knowing that such an investment would reap a rich harvest in sales, much greater than the $100,000 outlay. In 1973 Procter and Gamble spent about $221 million on TV, General Foods laid out about $110 million.[2] And both firms made lots of money that year. Certainly Hazel Bishop, a cosmetics firm, knows what impact TV has on the consumer. In 1950 when it started its TV campaign, the company sold $50,000 worth of products. Two years later the company had sales of $4.5 million, an increase of 9,000 percent; and there had been no change in the products themselves, and no advertising other than on television.[3] So you can understand why there were 79 percent more commercials on the air in 1970 than in

1960.[4] The advertisers know that television does a good job teaching what it shows.

Most people believe the TV ad, even many of those who claim in public they don't. Their actions in the supermarket usually prove the point. When confronted with having to choose between an advertised brand or an unadvertised brand, most people choose the one they've seen on TV.

Even professors of human behavior are influenced. Social psychologist Eliot Aronson, in his book *The Social Animal,* tells how he determines what to buy when he goes to the store: "Suppose I walk into a grocery store looking for a laundry detergent. I go to the detergent section and I am staggered by the wide array of brand names. Because it does not matter too much to me which one I buy, I may simply reach for one that is most familiar—and chances are it is familiar because I've heard and seen the name on TV commercials over and over again."[5]

A close friend of mine, a New Jersey gynecologist and surgeon, admits that he is swayed by commercials. One day he found himself in the paper-products section of a supermarket with his wife. He went to the toilet-paper shelf and squeezed a roll of Charmin toilet paper, the way those ladies do in the Charmin commercials, and tossed it and three more into the basket. He bought the Charmin product even though he has stock in Hudson and Kimberly-Clark paper companies, which also produce toilet paper. My friend's wife pointed out that her husband was not the only one who squeezed a roll of Charmin; several others were doing it while he was.

The advertising agencies that produce TV ads harbor no prejudices as to whom they try to sell. All segments of the human kingdom seem to be fair game, including little children.

Their efforts are part of no ideological conspiracy. Those who create TV advertising are not materialistic ideologists bent on converting viewers to their philosophy. In fact, they may go to church or synagogue regularly and even say grace at dinner every evening. But at work they are pragmatists, artful salesmen who view TV as a great gimmick to induce people to purchase products they are pushing. The fact that their efforts are turning children into materialists means nothing to them; the lines on a sales graph are what matters. The kids are viewed as a market, and the challenge is to exploit that market to the fullest. That means knowing how to overcome parental objections to the products they are promoting. It even means showing children how to wear down their parents' defense to the item the agency is trying to sell. This kind of psychic manipulation requires expert guidance. And advertising agencies get it—and pay well for it. Psychiatrists, psychologists, and sociologists are used to finding the right approach to selling kids consumer items. Some agencies have a motivation research department staffed by psychologists; others hire independent research firms, headed by psychologists, to provide the same service. Recruiting this kind of help is not difficult, for agency salaries and consultation fees are high. Advertising firms comb university campuses for motivational experts. But it is not a hit-and-miss kind of search. They can always check out the manual *A Directory of Social Scientists Interested in Motivation Research,* which lists available social scientists. Even the motivational research firms are easy to find. Most of them are listed—and there are hundreds of them—in *A Directory of Organizations Which Conduct Motivation Research.* Many of these firms are making big money. The Institute for Motivation Research, for example, reportedly grossed about $750,000 back in 1955 when TV was barely out of its crawling stage.[6]

The people who are putting together TV commercials, especially on a national level, consider what they are doing serious business. They are not interested in winning creativity or art awards. The trophy they seek is a more lucrative contract from a happy client. To achieve this end they must be on target. Consistency is required and to accomplish that means removing the guesswork from their efforts and becoming scientific in their approach. University graduate schools of business administration are helping to streamline the scientific approach; they are also producing bright young research and systems-oriented people for the advertising field, people who find it exciting to use the latest technology to make sure consumers chew their client's gum, wear their client's shirts, eat their client's cereal. In every marketing department of every major school of business, courses are offered on how to penetrate buyer defenses. One such course at the University of Massachusetts School of Business Administration is called "Buyer Behavior." Its catalogue description reads: "Analysis of buyer motivation and buying behavior. Explaining theories of consumer market behavior and models of decision-making process for *winning patronage.*"

There are college textbooks on how to sell products via TV. In them great emphasis is placed on finding the best method to develop sound selling ideas. Touching a viewer's emotions is stressed; taking advantage of his worries is implied.

In *The Television Commercial: Creativity and Craftsmanship,* there is an example that illustrates this point: "Most every good method . . . . begins with the acknowledgment of at least five basic human needs and wants. In their simplest forms, these are: shelter, food, clothing, appreciation and vanity.

"If these needs, one or all are not completely answered, a man will worry. Charles F. Adams, as Executive Vice-President, MacManus, John & Adams, Inc., puts it this way: 'People react from only two things other than instinct: ambition and worry. And of these two, worry is without question the more important motivation.' So here you have guidelines to finding selling ideas, the motivations inherent in man that need and seek satisfaction. If your product answers one or several of these needs, and does it better than competition, you will quickly find yourself on the trail of a persuasive selling idea."[7]

So students digest stuff like this and study hard to become experts in demonstrating how the products they will one day push on TV will eliminate viewer worries. We see on television how a certain brand of vitamin pills will overcome a skinny kid's worry of being a weakling; how a certain brand of sneakers will make a poorly coordinated boy into a great athlete.

The science of persuading humans to buy what is advertised is being documented in a scholarly fashion. Periodicals catering to both practitioners and educators in the advertising community can be found in university libraries across the country. They are packed with articles, many of them based on research studies, that provide techniques and tips on how to make certain kinds of products appealing to different ethnic groups, economic and social classes, and age levels. For example, in one issue of the *Journal of Advertising Research*, the author of the article "Communicating with Children," Rutgers University Psychology Professor William D. Wells offers advertising agency producers of TV commercials advice on how to reach preschool children:

"Children are literal and concrete minded. They do not handle abstractions well, and they are not adept at verbal associations. The moral is: show the product, show it big and show it doing something that meets a need."[8]

When Dr. Wells wrote this article he was also a consultant to the Benton and Bowles Inc. advertising agency.

The Ph.D.'s working in advertising tend to be thorough at their job, many of them constantly researching more effective ways of reaching the viewer. Joseph T. Plummer, who received his doctorate from Ohio State, is interested in commercials reaching the viewer's unconscious mind. In an article in *The Journal of Communication,* Dr. Plummer states there is evidence that viewers do respond unconsciously to commercials: "One indication that unconscious responses to advertising communication takes place may be seen in the physiological responses, such as galvanic skin response and heartbeat rate, that have been measured in the laboratory."[9]

He also noted that "significant pupil and skin response occur when the commercials present stimulating action, or extreme changes in the mood, tempo or volume of the commercial, or when there is some sexy event in the commercial."[10]

Plummer suggests that advertising communicators perfect reaching the viewer's unconscious mind when he writes: "Further research and experience with this level [unconscious] of response—often overlooked—is clearly needed in advertising."[11]

Advertising agencies know that in TV they have a medium that children, especially preschoolers, love, believe in, and trust. And they exploit the kids' attachment to TV.

The potency of television in conditioning youngsters to be loyal enthusiasts of a product, Vance Packard says in his *Hidden Persuaders,* whether they are old enough to

consume or not, became indisputable in the early fifties.

"A young New York ad man taking a marketing class at
a local university made the casual statement that, thanks
to TV, most children were learning to sing beer and other
commercials before learning to sing the 'Star Spangled
Banner.' "12

Mr. Packard adds: "Youth Research Institute, according to *Nation* [magazine], boasted that even five-year-
olds sing beer commercials 'over and over again with
gusto.' It pointed out that moppets not only sing the
merits of advertised products but do it with vigor displayed by the most raptly enthusiastic announcers and do
it all day long 'at no extra cost to the advertisers.' They
cannot be turned off as a set can.

"When at the beginning of the decade [fifties] television was in its infancy an ad appeared in a trade journal
alerting manufacturers to the extraordinary ability of TV
to etch messages on young brains. 'Where else on earth,'
the ad exclaimed, 'is brand consciousness fixed so firmly
in the minds of four-year-old tots? . . . . What is it
worth to a manufacturer who can close in on this juvenile
audience and continue to sell it under controlled conditions year after year, right up to its attainment of adulthood and full fledged buyer sta.,is? It can be done.
Interested?' "13

Before television, very little effort was made to sell
three, four, and five-year-olds via the mass media. Magazine and newspaper campaigns would have been a waste
since most preschoolers can't read; and radio was too
mystical a medium for kids to believe. But television is
obvious and you don't have to be able to read to be
reached by it. So advertisers found a way to crack a
market that seemed impenetrable. TV turned out to be a
vast gold mine which now seems bottomless. It is es-

timated that in 1971 children's television programming produced in excess of $75 million a year in advertising revenue for the commercial TV networks.[14] And most advertisers seem pleased with the results they have received from their TV ads.

Children's television advertising is a big business. And the people who are out to exploit the moppet market don't ease off because they are dealing with kids. They bring out every weapon in their arsenal: psychologists, researchers, sociologists, marketing specialists, artists, writers, actors, cameramen, producers, directors. Using the best equipment, they experiment and test until they feel certain they have found the approach that meets the commercial's objective, which is motivating the child to want the product they are pushing.

Certainly children, even their parents, are not aware of the brain power, energy, and time it takes to shape a commercial. They, for the most part, take TV for granted. Turn a knob or push a button and you get entertainment, news, escape. They view it as a pastime. Advertising agencies want to preserve this average viewer attitude toward TV. They don't want the viewer to know there are people they never see working in plush offices in Manhattan skyscrapers who are continually exploring ways to persuade children to do their bidding. These commercial-media hypnotists capitalize on children's basic openness, honesty, curiosity, and naïveté. The kids are their target. Children, pure hearted and wide eyed, soak in the messages they create, unable to screen the bad from the good. Defenseless, they sit captivated before their trusted friend and primary source of pleasure, the TV set, absorbing its offerings, becoming a part of a cycle which usually ends with the ringing of the advertiser's cash register. In 1968, advertising people estimated that 70 percent of the kids who watch TV ask their parents to buy products advertised on television and 89 percent of the parents do it.[15]

Many advertising men who are selling products to children consciously play on the parent-child relationship. Some openly admit it like Eugene Mahany, vice-president of Needham, Harper and Steers, a Chicago advertising agency: "We can shape our future marketing programs on what appeals directly to the child, not to the parent, because if the parent initiates the interest, then the appeal to the child is lessened, and the job of selling is made more difficult."[16]

This legitimized assault on our children is disturbing even to people who work in television. Mrs. Joan Ganz Cooney, the creator of *Sesame Street* and *Electric Company,* is aware of the injustice, the insensitivity, of allowing TV stations and networks to riddle our children with slick, captivating commercial messages. "If we, as a total society, put the interests of our children first, then we are led to the inescapable conclusion that it is terribly wrong to be pitching products—even high-quality products—at the young.

"It is like shooting fish in a barrel. It is grotesquely unfair. The target audience is, after all, illiterate, uneducated, unemployed, and hopelessly dependent on welfare from others."[17]

By watching most commercials our children are not only being brainwashed to want certain kinds of candy, toys, cookies, and cereals, they are on the receiving end of lies. Sam Sinclair Baker, who was an advertising man in New York for thirty years, exposes Madison Avenue's rationale for lying: "A lie that helps build profits is considered a permissible lie. Of course the lie must not be so blatant that it results in eventual damage to the company's profits . . . . A substantial amount of advertising is based on the concept of the permissible lie."[18]

Baker also mentions the damage this kind of legi-timized lying can cause: "This fakery, through saturation and repetition, undermines the attitudes and ethics of the adult, the child and the family."[19]

Many preschool children believe TV commercial mes-sages, whether they are lies or not. This could be psycho-logically damaging.

The commercial makers purposely lie and exaggerate to build their product's appeal. One way is to use special devices in the presentation of their messages. This can be done through camera angles, close-up photography, and speeded up action. In his 1971 study, *Saturday Chil-dren's Television*, Dr. F. Earle Barcus, professor of com-munications research at Boston University, cites some examples:

"1. Mattel doll ads (Dawn and Barbie dolls)—close-ups of dolls give an impression of large size with chil-dren almost always in the background.

2. Birdseye (Libbyland Dinners)—close-ups of sec-tions of the dinner with no objective criteria to judge size or quantity.

3. B. F. Goodrich (P. F. Flyer Shoes)—some of magi-cian Blackstone's magic tricks appear to be camera tricks instead.

4. Hasbro (Wacky Wheel)—Wheel appears to chase a man as if it had radar built in, and, as the announcer states, 'has a mind of its own.'

5. Kellogg's (Fruit Loops)—animation of sparkling sugar on cereal.

6. Marx (Big Wheel)—Action appears speeded up to make toy seem reckless and quite fast.

7. Mattel(Barbie Dolls)—'Live-action' dolls appear to be dancing by themselves when human manipula-tion is necessary. Also extreme close-ups of Barbie

'Grow Pretty Hair,' and 'Talking Barbie' make it
difficult to judge size of doll.

8. Mattel (Zoomer Boomer)—Quick editing, camera
    angles give impression of greater size and speed.

9. Pillsbury (Funny Face)—Close-ups and very close-
    ups of toy premium and when children are shown
    they are in background with a 'worms eye' view by
    the camera."[20]

Dr. Barcus found many other examples of the fairly
obvious use of special devices to sell products during the
nineteen-hour period he and his staff observed children's TV programming in the Boston area. "The point is
probably not so much the exact proportion of commercials which use these techniques," he states, "but rather
that there are enough obvious ones which may well
mislead the child into believing things about products to
cause some concern."[21]

Obtaining a product that doesn't do what television
says it does could disappoint a child and cause a painful
conflict in his mind: he wonders how television—something he loves—can lie to him. In some respects it is like a parent who yells at a child or spanks him
for no apparent reason. The child continues to love his
parent, but is emotionally hurt because of the unjust
actions of the parent. It is all very bewildering to him.

The conflict intensifies when the disappointing TV
commercial experience is repeated. The pattern takes its
toll: Some children, deeply attached to TV, become like
cigarette smokers who continue to smoke even though
they know it is physically harmful. The child continues to
watch TV commercials and continues to be sold, disap-
pointments notwithstanding. These kids are hooked.
The agencies know it and show no mercy.

There are other kids who have been fooled by TV
commercials, but they have avoided being trapped. They

fight back. But what happens to them, in a way, is tragic also. They become cynical, negative, self-centered, even hostile. Those who become hostile turn rebellious and want to lash out at the society that has taken advantage of their openness, their trust. Many others scrap whatever idealism they possessed and become preoccupied with survival, concentrating most of their energy and time in practicing living life as if it were a "dog-eat-dog" existence, the way their parents have been forced to live.

Advertisers and their agencies are not concerned about the psychological wreckage they create in the minds of the little tots who watch TV. In fact, they not only want to persuade children to purchase their products, they want to mold them into life-long users of their products. Clyde Miller, in his *Process of Persuasion,* articulates the advertiser's ultimate dream: ". . . if you expect to be in business for any length of time, think of what it can mean to your firm in profits if you can condition a million or ten million children who will grow up as adults trained to buy your product as soldiers trained to advance when they hear the trigger words 'forward march.' "[22]

This kind of conditioning is widely practiced on television, the medium that opened up the children's market, the medium that many kids believe and trust.

Today the TV commercial is a part of a child's life. It is as natural to him as the sunrise.

When a group of fifth and sixth graders in a Chesterfield, Massachusetts, school were asked to create a TV program, they never considered not including commercials. They produced three of them, all a lot more creative than the program itself.

The commercial has been woven into the American child's consciousness and television is the instrument that did the job.

The present condition of children's TV commercials

raises serious moral questions: (1) Should advertisers, advertising agencies, and the commercial television industry have the kind of freedom they enjoy now to penetrate and fashion the psyches of children, possibly for life? (2) Considering the hypnotic effect TV has on many people, should TV be used as virtually an open marketplace for advertisers to sell their wares?

Obviously, the child—especially the preschooler—needs help to keep from being hooked by the television commercial. The government could help. For example, Congress could ban all advertising on children's television. But considering the political and economic climate of our country, the chances of that happening in the foreseeable future are slim. A more realistic approach would be to limit advertising to institutional announcements. In other words, at the beginning and conclusion of a program an announcer would read something like this over a slide: "This program was made possible through a grant from ABCD Corporation."

Madison Avenue and TV industry resistance to institutional advertising would be stiff, setting off a battle that would take years to resolve. There are two other alternatives: One is to limit commercials to before the start and after the end of a show. The purpose of this arrangement would be to keep advertisers from being associated with shows. They would buy spots before and after a show—never the program. The other alternative is for networks and TV stations to lump all commercials in one ten-minute segment during each hour. This kind of an arrangement would be helpful to parents, because they would know when commercials would be aired, giving them greater control over their children's commercial watching. Some parents might find it convenient to turn off the set during that ten-minute segment. Of course, the commercials on either proposed TV advertising scheme would have to meet more demanding standards than they do now. Absolutely no deception, subterfuge, sexism, racism, violence, sexiness, or sadism should be allowed.

Proposing an idea to the broadcasting industry is a lot easier than having it accepted and implemented, especially if it involves emptying treasure from the industry's chest. So the prospects that the policy makers of television commercials will adopt either one of the alternatives are very poor. Even if they showed some interest in adopting one, it would take years before it would be structured into a television program and commercial schedule, and while TV men pondered the merit of a plan, millions of children would continue to be commercially brainwashed—just as they are now. The challenge is to repulse the TV advertising assault on children immediately.

The parent has the power to do that. Mind you, it is not easy, because it requires time and patience and sensitivity. But think of the reward to both parents and children, for it could mean snatching a child away from the clutches of a commercial monster masquerading as a friend who is full of fun.

Satu Repo, a Canadian education writer and editor, who is also a parent, found the time and patience to free her daughters from the spell of the TV commercial: "I attempted to undermine their faith in commercials by pointing out that this and that product was really quite different from what the man said on TV. It never cut any ice with them until once when they were inspired to do some testing on their own hook. They were watching a commercial on All Bran cereal, which was reputed to have unusually fine qualities in taste, food value, etc.

One of the twins remembered that we had a box of the stuff in our cupboard and she brought it into the living room to taste it. 'It tastes like dried-up grass,' she said very indignantly and gave a sample to her sister, who agreed with her. The next afternoon I caught them in the kitchen having a very heated discussion with some of their friends. Sylvia and Marya (our daughters) were maintaining that TV commercials lied, and the other kids did not believe them. It ended up with my girls passing around the All Bran box. After munching it quietly for a few minutes the kids had to admit that it tasted like dried up grass, irrespective of what the nice man said on the screen. I don't know whether this was a revelation to the other kids in the neighborhood, but it seemed to have a lasting impact on Sylvia and Marya. They no longer were pushing for Name Brand products."[23]

The secret to Mrs. Repo's success was that she did not nag her daughters, she gently challenged the credibility of the TV ads while in their presence, time and time again. She took advantage of her children's innate curiosity without alienating them. Mrs. Repo's gracious persistence helped to motivate her girls to make the investigation on their own.

Of course, though a heavy responsibility rests with the parents in weaning their children from TV commercials, organized public pressure must continue to be applied on the TV industry and federal government to clean up the children's TV commercial mess.

13

TV Can Stunt
Healthy Growth

Parents do their children a disservice by allowing them to watch too much TV, even if the programs are all educational. Dr. Urie Bronfenbrenner, the noted human developmentalist, explains why: ". . . as presently employed, television contributes to the alienation of children by placing both them and their parents in the passive role of the viewer. From this point of view, the primary danger of the television screen lies not so much in the behavior it produces as the behavior it prevents —the talks, the games, the family festivities, and arguments through which much of the child's learning takes place and his character is formed. Turning on the television set can turn off the process that transforms children into people."[1]

Sitting glued to the tube during most of his waking hours could warp a young child's social and emotional development. He learns that having a good time is turning on the set and spending hours before it, seldom uttering a word or acknowledging the presence of another human being in the room. If his TV-viewing habits are not altered, the child could easily grow into an adult incapable of communicating with others. He becomes an uncaring human being, immersed in what TV tells him is how he is supposed to feel.

A daily dose of long uninterrupted periods before the set could also dull a child's ability to fantasize and be creative, as he learns to rely more and more on television's ready-made fantasies, thus blocking his natural pull to make believe, to enact his daydreams, to invent games spontaneously. Children need this kind of creative outlet, for it is an expression of self. It is a necessary exercise for the development of self-esteem.

A young child's knowledge of the world is primarily visual. What he sees he believes. But seeing is not enough. A child also wants to touch, to explore what he has seen. A young habitual TV watcher usually sees a lot but rarely gets to touch or explore what he's seen, leaving him unfulfilled, a condition he is not consciously aware of, but which could take its toll in poor behavioral development. I have observed that the young child who is a heavy television watcher tends to lack volition, is not a self-starter, is more comfortable being led than leading, and usually feels happier and safer in front of a TV set than in a room full of people.

Psychologists Richard Held and Alan Hein carried out an experiment in 1963 which demonstrated what happens to the young when they do not have an opportunity to explore, to manipulate their world. They worked with two sets of kittens for six weeks. The young cats were kept in the darkness for all but two hours a day. During those two hours, one set of kittens were wheeled around in a carriage, left in a passive state where their situation was controlled by an outside force. The other set of kittens were allowed to explore their environment freely. At the end of the experiment, the active kittens' development was normal. The passive set of kittens, however, were perceptually and behaviorally underdeveloped. It took considerable exploration before the abnormally developing kittens caught up to the other kittens.[2]

Children learn by doing. Flipping on a light switch, turning on a faucet, opening up an umbrella, banging a nail into a piece of wood, pouring water into a glass, climbing a tree, and even falling from it are activities that help to develop a child's motor skills and they are learning experiences as well. By having an opportunity to explore, children learn to master their environment, understanding how to negotiate physical problems like climbing over a fence or opening a cellar door; by playing with other children they learn to deal socially; they also learn to appreciate the difference between safe and dangerous situations, which sometimes is learned by experimenting.

Very young children are curious. They do not need much motivation. They are interested in how things work, what they are and what can be done to them or with them. For parents to plunk their preschooler before a TV set for several hours during a time when they could be playing and exploring could stunt their child's curiosity and motor development. A parent should provide the kind of environment for the child where his curiosity heightens, his motor skills grow, he learns to sort, build, fill, empty, open, shut, fit in and take out. He needs materials to do all of that and also to mess with materials like paint and clay. He needs dolls, or animals to dress, undress, wash, dry, spank, yell at, and soothe. If a child spends most of his free time watching television, he loses the precious opportunity to learn by doing.[3]

At this point it is important to make clear that abstinence from television is no guarantee of healthy motor, emotional, and behavioral development in a child. Too much TV is the crippler, not television itself. There are good things on television, and denying a child access to them is depriving him culturally. Parents must be balanced, exposing their children to healthy TV programming but never allowing TV to interfere with their need to explore, to fantasize, to create, to learn by doing.

But to be an effective parent requires more than balance. Creativity or a knack for securing creative help is needed. Creativity is needed to establish new entertainment and play habits that are not centered around television. It means finding substitute activities for televiewing.

A number of things can be done that won't cost much money. Take preschoolers, for example. Most of them spend lots of time watching TV in the morning and in the afternoon. A way to keep the child from watching the tube in the morning is to invite one of his or her friends to the house through lunch time. It is important, of course, that the two kids play in a stimulating environment, because they could easily drift over to the television set. By a stimulating environment, I mean a play area where there are games, crayons, paper, books, dolls, and balls—in other words, objects which can be used by the kids to create fun situations. Children remember fun situations and want to repeat that kind of experience. The more they repeat it, the less interest they'll show in morning TV. Certainly, having two children in the house all morning can be somewhat of a hardship to a parent. But if the play area is an exciting place, the children will most likely spend most of their time there and won't get in the way of the parent's housework.

Having a child over every morning to play with your child could become too harrowing an experience for a parent. A way to get around that problem is to work out an arrangement with the parents of your child's friend whereby you take turns minding each other's child. This kind of a deal would provide the parent with a personal benefit: a couple of free days during the week.

After lunch most preschoolers take a nap which lasts about an hour. When the child awakes, the parent could take him for a walk or could read the child a story or play a game with him. By mid-afternoon, he should be ready to watch *Sesame Street* and *Mr. Rogers Neighborhood.* And that should be the extent of the preschooler's exposure to TV from Monday through Friday unless a special like *Peter Pan* or *The Wizard of Oz* is on. A check through the *TV Guide* should provide a parent with information on upcoming specials that would be of interest to three, four, and five-year-olds. On Sunday, kids could benefit from programs like *The World of Disney* and *Wild Kingdom.*

Saturday morning, of course, is traditional TV kiddie time, which means the channels are choked with cartoons and commercials that are engineered to make the child viewer a surrogate salesman of the products that are being pushed. Most of the shows are inferior forms of entertainment that not only lack value but sometimes glorify violence, ridicule parents, and demonstrate many other forms of antisocial behavior. But millions of kids watch, nevertheless. For many of them Saturday morning TV serves the function of their favorite toy or game.

But one of the major functions of a toy or game is to prepare and teach a child to cope with life as an adult. The toy or game gives him a glimpse of many of the possible situations he will have to face and roles he will have to assume in later life. Unfortunately, much of what most kids watch on Saturday mornings, or for that matter the rest of the week, gives a child a warped idea of adulthood. Muscle, cunning, conning, and sexual triumph are stressed. Children absorb values of a troubled society and idealize TV adult models who are not fit to deal with the kinds of problems most adults face daily.

Another major function of toys and games is to help stimulate a child's imagination, to open up and activate the creative problem-solving process of his mind. With a few exceptions, TV fails in this area, for its purpose is to imagine for the viewer and solve the problems it establishes.

In most of the cartoons and detective and western episodes he watches, the child knows that whatever problems arise during the program they are sure to be solved in less than thirty minutes. So he becomes conditioned to expect thirty-minute solutions and most likely will carry that kind of expectation into adult life.

Toys and games are supposed to stimulate individual and group participation in the creative learning process called "play." There isn't much physical play in a home on Saturday mornings when the kids are lying around the set being involved in television.

In most homes, Saturday morning is when parents sleep later than usual, and children rule the TV set, picking up bad behavior and attitudes and neglecting the human development needs of learning by doing and exploring.

Parents who really care about their kids will give up that extra hour's sleep so they can participate in some planned activity with their preschool children on Saturday morning. It is a great opportunity for the father who works all week and doesn't get to see much of his children. He can devote a couple of undivided hours of attention and affection to his little ones. He can take a walk in the woods and answer his child's questions about trees, flowers, birds, and squirrels and chipmunks; he can take the child to a playground, play ball with him, push him on a swing, and just be there to catch him when he reaches the end of his slide. Museums, aquariums, zoos are good places to take children on a Saturday morning. So are lakes, an ocean front, a farm. Canoeing, hiking, fishing, a ride in the country can be fun too. A simple thing like a bus ride can be a lot of fun to a preschooler, especially if he is with a parent who is with him in spirit as well as body. So many parents these days spend time with their children because they feel obligated to be with them. Children can sense when their parents' thoughts are not trained on them but are elsewhere, perhaps at work, back home, the golf course, the clubhouse. By being alone with his child, a father has an opportunity to build a beautiful bond with him, which could last both their lifetimes. Besides, a child needs genuine communications experiences with his parents, where he is alone with them, in a happy setting, and he feels unafraid to share his fears, bewilderments, and worries and to express his joys and dreams. The communications experience is more than a verbal exchange, it is touching each other, embracing each other; it is allowing love to flow freely toward each other. This kind of experience is a vital part of a child's education. When a child knows he can really talk to his parents he becomes a secure human being. He knows where his major source of support is. And because of this he usually learns well, is less concerned about his shortcomings, has a fairly good understanding of himself, and possesses a zest for knowing about all of the things that he sees—and he sees a lot more than the child who is introverted, timid, and insecure. A secure child's emotional, intellectual, even physical growth is usually sound.

But the child who spends every Saturday morning a captive of TV cartoons usually misses the human communications experience that only a flesh-and-blood parent can provide. Television becomes his most de-

pendable "parent." At least it is consistent, always providing him with fun. But children cannot live by television alone!

When many school children come home, they turn on
the set until supper. Some even watch while eating
supper, turning it off only before going to bed. This kind
of pastime is not healthy. The child surrenders himself to
television, doing what it demands, which usually means
being attentive to its messages. This kind of situation is
certainly not conducive to releasing and developing
one's human potentialities. And that's what a six, seven,
eight, nine, ten, and eleven-year-old should be busy
doing. Television takes you to exotic places, introduces
you to exciting people and involves you in unusual
situations, but it doesn't develop those latent human
qualities of integrity, honesty, compassion, and love. It
doesn't cultivate creativity or sharpen the mind. Nor can
it search a human soul. All of which requires volition. TV
takes more than it gives. And if parents are not vigilant, it
will rob their children of most of their energy and time.
Mothers and fathers of school children must guard
against losing their children to television. If they lose
them—and most parents are unaware of how to spot this
condition—their children's development could be im-
paired.

How can a parent tell when his child is lost to TV? A
fairly reliable sign is when a child spends most of his time
before the tube.

There are reasons why school children gravitate
toward television, reasons besides the medium's mag-
netic pull. According to a study done for the U.S. Surgeon
General, school children watch TV for entertainment, to
relax, or to relieve loneliness.[4] In drawing their children
away from the set, parents could use that study's findings
as a guide. For example, they should simply provide new

entertainment opportunities for their children and other means of relaxation, and perhaps more parental attention would be a way of overcoming a child's loneliness. And attention doesn't always have to be in the form of hugs and kisses, although those should be given; it also means providing a child with an opportunity to play with other kids, to travel to different places, and to meet different people. In essence, it means parents taking the time and energy to develop a stimulating play phase in a kid's life and involving themselves in his interests and aspirations so that they are close to the child's feelings and are around to provide some solace when that is needed.

School children should be allowed to watch more TV than preschoolers. But only about thirty minutes more a day, and most of their watching should take place after supper. Their afternoons following school should be a time for play, for hobby development, and not a period devoted to television gazing. Playing with other children is very important to a child's social development. When he is with other kids, he is learning how to work in a group, how to give and take, how to meet defeat, how to handle triumph, how to preserve friendships. He experiences the emotions of liking and disliking. In other words, he is preparing for the day when he has to deal as an adult in the outside world. A child who locks himself in a TV room all afternoon will most likely be socially maladjusted as an adult.

If a child lives in a neighborhood where there aren't any children in his age range, parents should find a group of kids for their child to play with, even if it means transporting the child across town.

Determining the child's playmates should rest with the child. Often a child has a few close friends in school. The parent should find out who they are. If the child is a first or second grader, the parent should phone the parents of his school chums to work out a get-together. Perhaps an arrangement could be established whereby kids switch playing sites, one day at one guy's home, the next day at the other guy's home.

Children eight years old and older should do their own phoning and playmate arranging, and the parents should provide the transportation, if that is necessary.

Of course, many parents don't have the means to transport their child across town. They could take their child to the neighborhood playground or park—a place that usually attracts lots of kids, or the child could join a recreation department baseball, basketball, or soccer team. If parents don't know about the recreation department's weekday after-school program for children, they should phone the department to see what is available for their child.

Between three P.M. and five P.M. Monday through Friday is a good time for school children to pursue a hobby that is based on a deep interest. For example, a youngster who is fascinated with space travel, the stars, and other planets, and is curious about the way our solar system operates, should be introduced to astronomy and rocketry. And the child doesn't have to attend university lectures to acquaint himself with those two areas. On the other hand, parents shouldn't eliminate that possibility, especially after the child's knowledge of astronomy and rocketry grows.

There are many things parents can do to help their child pursue his hobby. For instance, the youngster who is interested in astronomy and rocketry could be taken on periodic trips to the planetarium, even subscribe to the planetarium's newsletter, which lists different programs. If there are no planetariums nearby, perhaps parents could plan a trip to the nearest one. The child could build spaceship models, ones that actually fly, and create a clay model of our solar system or better yet, construct a moving model of the system. He could be taken on weekly trips to the library to pick up books and magazines. The child could subscribe to periodicals that specialize in astronomy and rocketry. He could keep a scrapbook on those two areas of interest and the child's hobby could be woven into his school curriculum; his parents could tell his teacher about their son's interest in astronomy and rocketry and ask the teacher to weave it into his school work.

Parents should be more than chauffeurs and purchasers while involved in their children's hobbies. They should encourage their children to pursue their interests and offer guidance and help when asked; they should acknowledge their children's hobby achievements with praise.

By turning their child's deep interest into a hobby, parents are recognizing at least some of their child's potentialities and helping him develop them.

Scheduling hobby work could be sticky. Some kids might find their hobby so fascinating that they would want to spend all of their time working at it. Socially, this kind of vertical concentration could be harmful to the child, for a child needs to interact with his peers. On the other hand, the child's enthusiasm shouldn't be squelched. One solution to this problem is to find other children who have the same hobby. The child who has an interest in astronomy and rocketry, for example, might get together with other kids who have the same interest and work on projects with them.

Perhaps the parents could set aside one or two afternoons for hobby development, so that the child could spend the three other afternoons playing with friends or participating in sports.

As for keeping school-age children from watching too

much TV on weekends, the approach offered for pre-schoolers could be adapted for older children.

In offering ways to keep children from watching too much television, I am not suggesting, overtly or subtly, that parents ban television watching. I am pointing out, though, that excessive televiewing by children could rob them of those precious growing up moments when they are supposed to be learning how to relate to other human beings, when they are supposed to be learning by doing, when they are supposed to be exploring the world around them.

14

A Factor in the American Family Breakup

"The American family" is a popular theme on TV and radio and in newspapers and magazines. It is also a silent and painful daydream topic of thousands of unhappy husbands and wives, disgruntled and bewildered parents, and confused and hurting children.

What is happening to family unity? Why don't we communicate better with each other? Why don't our children listen to us? Why don't our parents understand us? What's wrong with our family?

Those are questions that many family members ask, more often to themselves than to anyone else. But because they don't verbalize their puzzlement and their torment does not mean they are willing to endure their condition. Many married couples split up without ever knowing exactly why; many children run away from home without ever telling their parents why and without ever really understanding themselves why they fled. And there are those in many families who don't flee to the hills, but who emotionally cut themselves off from certain members of their family or from everyone in the family.

The American family is in trouble. Divorce rates are higher than ever before. In 1972, four out of every ten marriages ended in divorce. Parent and child communications are steadily deteriorating. And there does not seem to be any let up in the family breakdown process. Mainly because another process is intertwined with it: the emancipation of the American woman, something that has long been overdue and will have to take its course. A year? Five years? Ten years? No one can accurately predict. But one thing is certain—the American mother, who traditionally has been the backbone of the American family, is questioning practices and standards she once took for granted. She is rebelling and her husband is perplexed. The children are caught in the crossfire.

As in most struggles for independence and self-identity, both sides overreact. The men, conditioned to live in a male-dominated society, recoil at feminist expressions, especially those which evolve from rhetoric to action. Women, on the other hand, finally feel free to grapple with their true emotions and thoughts, and show little tolerance for men's resentment of what they term "female aggressiveness." Two forces are pitted against each other, with the old resisting the new, setting off friction and at times flame, which disrupts and destroys.

Television has *not* helped the situation. Since TV reflects the condition of our society, watching television reinforces the condition in the viewer. It seeps in, presses in a little more every time we watch, until we are incapable of distinguishing between the condition and ourselves. So TV heightens the battle of the sexes without our knowing it. The struggle for women's emancipation is continually drilled at us while we watch the news—through commercials that urge women to "do their thing" and soap operas featuring characters who have exchanged the dress for blue jeans and the bra for "what comes naturally." "You've come a long way, baby" has become a reminder for them to keep up the fight for equality and independence.

Television has contributed in other ways to the American family dilemma. The daily barrage of commercials has made us more self-conscious, more self-centered, and less other-concerned. Even members of our family receive less genuine attention and affection because of our preoccupation with smelling sweet, having dry armpits, having that wholesome, natural look, looking young, and having the pep of a youth.

The "you only live once" theme is continually drummed at the adult viewer, making many of them panicky, fearing that they are running out of time. So they launch a crusade to recapture their youth, to do the things they have been missing out on, to make every moment of life pleasurable, to live out their secret dreams—and swing, "be free."

The drive of parents for complete physical fulfillment becomes so intense that they abandon their homes, their spouses, and their children and run off to find their fountain of youth or nirvana. Of course, not all parents who are swept up in "doing their thing" run away. They stick it out feeling very sorry for themselves, having difficulty hiding their displeasure, frustration, and bitterness. All of this is communicated nonverbally to the rest of the family and barriers rise between family members. However, there are others who stick it out, spending as little time as possible at home; they simply use their home as a resting stop between escapades. In both of these situations, parents see less and less of their children, who, in turn, see more and more of TV. The kids resent the lack of attention from their flesh-and-blood parents and choose new parents from television fare.

Many of them develop a strong attachment to their electronic parents, continually comparing them with their real mothers and fathers. Usually, their adopted parents fare better in the comparison, and the barriers between family members thicken.

There are still many parents who have successfully resisted TV's temptings to join the "now generation." But they are beginning to notice cracks in their family's solidarity. The parent and child seem to be drifting farther apart; there are longer periods of silence between family members. Days may go by without an exchange of more than a couple of sentences. In spirit, many of these family households operate as a rooming house; everyone keeps to himself, rarely sharing any of his experiences, concerns, fears, or joys.

Regular daily television watching, in large measure, is to blame for this condition. Parents and children surrender most of their free time to the tube. It saps their vitality; it dominates their consciousness.

Television is helping to kill that great American tradition—the family meal. In many homes across the land, families may be in the same room eating but they are not really together, because while shoveling food into their mouth they have their eyes and consciousness trained on the TV tube. In other homes during mealtime, family members are scattered about the house mechanically devouring a TV dinner while seated before a television set, totally absorbed in the action they see.

In the past, the family meal was a time when father, mother, and children shared their daily experiences, told stories, swapped jokes, and pitched in to help some family member who had a problem. By participating in the family meal, children learned a great deal. They observed the different roles played by their parents and brothers and sisters during the family meal. This helped them to appreciate how each member fit into the family unit. They also learned to appreciate some of their parents' problems—an insight which inspired them to volunteer to help out more around the house.

The family meal was a time when family members learned to share home responsibilities like cleaning up after eating; it was a time for building togetherness and tightening family unity.

Dr. Urie Bronfenbrenner, professor of human development and family studies and psychology at Cornell, thinks television disrupts healthy family interaction. "Like a sorcerer of old, the television set casts its magic spell—freezing speech and action, and turning the living into silent statues so long as the enchantment lasts."[1]

The trouble is, there is always more of the electronic magic to come and the more the TV-watching ritual settles into the family pattern of life, the more estranged family members become toward each other and the tele-viewing habit grows more and more into an addiction. It is as if TV, like a viper, draws from the habitual viewer his love, compassion, and other emotions, leaving him emotionally drained, unequipped to interact with deep feeling with other people.

Some children's television programming is destroying child-and-parent bonds in many American homes. In more and more shows, parents are being portrayed as fools, buffoons, and fumbling and bumbling boobs. Watching Saturday morning TV is like experiencing "Ridicule Your Mom and Dad Day."

The parental models presented on popular children's shows like the *Barkleys, Jetsons, Bugs Bunny, Flintstones,* and *Bewitched* are dangerous. Many kids identify with the kid characters on those shows and unconsciously adopt their style of relating to their parents and become sassy, sarcastic, and disobedient.

A few random samples from network TV fare during a couple of Saturdays in February 1973: On the *Barkleys*, the kids in the show rarely listen to their father. In one segment, the father asks his son not to push a button, but the kid does it anyway. On the program *Jetsons*, the father in the show is made out to be a weak, half-witted, indecisive character. In one episode, the Jetson daughter wins a song contest. Since the young lady is a celebrity, television comes to the Jetsons' home to interview her. The father is beside himself, nervous, feeble, and about to pass out. Finally, Dad pulls himself together only to realize that he made another mistake: he had allowed his teenage daughter to go out on a date with Jetstreamer, a famous swinging rock singer. The father catches up to the couple and proceeds to embarrass his daughter and ends up being a star of a rock concert. Part of the moral of the story is that fathers are ridiculously overgrown children. The *Bugs Bunny* show takes jabs at parents also. The cartoon called "Who's Kitten Who," for example, was a sarcastic dig at parental authority and an exhibition of a child's superior attitude toward his father. Sylvester, one of the major characters in the cartoon, tells his son that it's time they discussed the "tricks in the trade" and the son replies, "Yes Dad, what is it you'd like to know?" When the father is unable to catch a mouse, the son turns to his father and says, "What kind of father are you anyhow?" Disgusted, the son says, "Now I'm afraid to show my face in public."

Fred, who plays the role of the father in the *Flintstones*, is the laughingstock of the show. He is made out to be a dumb, loud-mouthed character, continually tripping over himself.

On *Bewitched*, Darin, the show's father and husband is the butt of practically every joke, always being laughed at. He gets blamed for everyone else's blunders and rarely speaks up to protest this kind of abuse.

Even *Kid Power,* generally a good show which deals with some deep concerns children have, has an anti-parent orientation. The kid characters in the show are portrayed as people who are equipped to solve all of their problems without any adult help—an unrealistic and dangerous concept, because children need adult guidance just to survive. Leading kids to believe they could negotiate life alone at the age of four, five, six, and seven undermines the child-parent relationship. Instead of bringing his problems to his parents, the child may first try to solve them himself, possibly hurting himself physically and psychologically in the process.

The program's attempt to deal with racism is admirable, but it doesn't always handle the problem wisely. For example, in one episode the kid characters attack parents for harboring prejudices against blacks, Russians, and others. The only trouble with this kind of approach is that while it combats one set of prejudices it unwittingly plants the seeds of another prejudice in the mind of the child viewer: a prejudice against parents.

Continual exposure to television's put down of parents could easily turn children against their parents without either the children or the mothers and fathers knowing the cause of the antagonism. It is simply a case of the kids being brainwashed. Not understanding the cause of the difficulty forces parents to resort to unjust and harsh action, which only compounds the family fracture. Parental lashing out hurts all parties concerned. The children don't understand why they are being punished and parents develop deep guilt feelings for striking their children.

The future of the American family? According to Dr. Lawrence Freidman, a Los Angeles family specialist and psychiatrist, the immediate future looks bleak. He feels

TV has already taken its toll of the people who will be the mothers and fathers of the next generation of families: "Our teenagers have grown up watching TV steadily. Because of this, they have everything except the ability to relate to other humans. These 'TV orphans' will be the adult divorce statistics of tomorrow."[2]

Attorney Sid Siller, a prominent New York City divorce specialist, recognizes TV's capacity to erode family unity, to destroy marriages, but his forecast is more hopeful than Dr. Freidman's: "I know from my own practice just how destructive TV is to marriage. I've seen many couples who simply had lost their ability to communicate with each other, even though they were sitting side by side watching TV through the years of marriage.

"But I do see some hope for the future. We can curb the spiraling divorce rate if we can just educate young people to the dangers of TV."[3]

15

The Set Is *Not* a Toy: It Bites

When the Andersons' cat started convulsing, they rushed her to the veterinarian. Their previous cat had the same symptoms before she died. At first, the Andersons thought the animal had been chewing on electric wire and had been severely shocked. That is what they thought happened to their first cat. When Dr. Vogel checked the cat's mouth and the rest of her body and saw no signs of burns, he, at first, was at a loss to explain the cause of the convulsions. Finally, he recalled an article he had read concerning the effect television had on a group of dogs. Dr. Vogel then asked the Andersons if their cat spent much time near their television set. When they said she did, he asked the couple if their first cat had rested near the set also. She had, the Andersons said, in fact, close to the spot where their present cat curls up. Dr. Vogel's prescription: keep the cat from resting too close to the television set. The Andersons have followed his advice and the cat is no longer suffering convulsions.

As for the article Dr. Vogel referred to, it appeared in the Spring 1972 issue of the *Veterinary Record,* a British publication. In it, Dr. James Cunningham tells of dogs that started convulsing after spending considerable time near a "turned on" television set. When the set was removed the convulsions ended.[1]

Dr. John Ott's experiments at the Environmental Health and Light Research Institute in Sarasota, Florida, provides additional evidence that radiation emission from television could hurt animal life. After noticing unusual results in his experiments with plant life, he decided to run the test on rats. Dr. Ott described his experiments in the *Journal of Learning Disabilities* in 1968: "Two rats approximately three months old were placed in each of two cages directly in front of the color television tube and the set was turned on for six hours each weekday and ten hours on Saturday and Sunday. One cage was placed in front of the half of the tube covered with black photographic paper and the other cage in front of the lead shielding which was one-eighth inch in thickness....The rats protected only with black paper showed stimulated abnormal activities from three to ten days and then became progressively lethargic. At 30 days they were extremely lethargic and it was necessary to push them to make them move about the cage. The rats shielded with the lead showed somewhat similar abnormal behavior patterns but to a very considerably lesser degree and more time was required before these abnormal behavior patterns became apparent. This experiment was repeated three times and the same results were obtained."[2]

Dr. Ott noticed in another experiment that excessive exposure to color TV affected the rats' sex life: "When the color television set was placed in the greenhouse area of our laboratory the location was 15 feet from our animal breeding room with two ordinary building partitions in between. We observed that immediately following placing the color television set in the greenhouse our animal breeding program, which had been going on very successfully for over two years, was completely disrupted and whereas litters of rats had previously averaged eight or twelve or more young, this immediately dropped off to one or two and many of these did not survive. After removal of the TV set approximately six months' time was required before the breeding program was back to normal."[3]

In another study, Dr. Ott discovered evidence supporting his theory that X-ray emission could influence the endocrine system, producing abnormal physical and mental activity over an extended period of time.[4]

Obviously, what affects cats, dogs, and rats might not affect humans. On the other hand, anatomically, we do have something in common: flesh, bone, glands, and blood, composed of billions of cells. There is evidence that radiation can damage cells in animals and humans. Perhaps humans have a greater tolerance for radiation emission than cats, dogs, and rats, perhaps it takes longer for radiation to disrupt the physiological balance in humans. But a tolerance level has its limit. Besides, there's always the possibility that the person who watches TV more than four hours a day, up close to the set, may have already sustained considerable internal bodily damage without knowing it, attributing whatever ails him to the latest "bug" that seems to be sweeping the neighborhood.

Back in 1964, two U.S. Air Force physicians went to the American Academy of Pediatrics in New York City to reveal a strange medical case in which both men participated. They had noticed thirty children suffering from the same symptoms: nervousness, continuous fatigue, headaches, loss of sleep, vomiting. The usual tests for infections and childhood illness were made. Nothing positive showed up. The food and water supplies in the area were checked. Both were clean. After talking to the parents and the children, the doctors discovered that the thirty boys and girls were heavy television watchers, spending three to six hours a day in front of the tube during the week and six to ten hours on Saturdays and Sundays.

The doctors ordered a total abstinence from TV. In the twelve homes where the parents complied with the physicians' instructions, the children's symptoms vanished in two to three weeks. In the other homes, where the parents cut TV viewing to about two hours a day, the children's symptoms took a longer time to disappear: five to six weeks. A couple of months later, eleven children came down with the same symptoms. It turned out that their parents were ignoring the doctors' orders and their kids were spending as much time before the picture tube as they did when they were ushered into the doctors' office feeling sick.[5]

There is no concrete proof that exposure to excessive amounts of TV radiation caused the children's illness. But it is a fact that TV sets give off radiation, color television more than black and white. It is also a fact that excessive radiation can make humans sick. How much exposure will hurt humans? TV set manufacturers think they know the safety level. But then, do they know if TV watching is as safe for heavy users as it is for light users? Parents should know the answer to that question for the protection of their children and themselves.

Not every set that rolls off the assembly line is safe; some leak more radiation than others. For example, in a Public Health Service survey of five thousand color TV sets in Suffolk County, New York, in 1969, 20 percent of those sets emitted X-rays at a level above the maximum safe limit. The Health Service released the report to the public and urged all color television set owners to sit at least six to ten feet away from their sets to minimize potential radiation hazards.[6] Normally thousands of children sit so close to their color sets that they can touch the tube, and this goes on without their parents' knowing—or caring.

Shortly after General Electric admitted that some of its sets were emitting some X-rays, the U.S. Surgeon General's office launched an investigation. It found that the GE incident was not an isolated case, that X-ray emission seemed to be an industry-wide problem.[7] Consumer advocate Ralph Nader's investigation substantiated the Surgeon General's findings.

Radiation exposure is only one possible health hazard to TV watchers. Eyesight damage is possibly another. The American Optometric Association recommends watching television in a softly illuminated room. "When the room is totally dark," the AOA warns, "the contrast between the television screen and the surrounding area is too great for comfortable and efficient vision."[8] Heavy television viewing, some ophthalmologists feel, can cause severe eye strain. If a child's eyes water while watching TV it is a sign of visual discomfort and it may mean he needs professional care; close concentration on the TV screen for a long period of time may result in general fatigue, the AOA warns.

A Japanese ophthalmologist's study showed that televiewing at incorrect distances for more than an hour slows down the ability to fix one's vision on a stationary object. He has recommended that the optimum distance to sit from the television screen is about seven times the diameter of the screen. This particular guidance, incidentally, is included in the television manuals of Japanese television sets; no such directions are included in American manuals.[9]

The American Optometric Association, which has

looked into effects of TV watching on eyesight, provides
seven rules for television viewing:
—Make sure your television set is properly installed
and the antenna properly adjusted.
—Place the set to avoid glare or reflections from lamps,
windows, or other bright sources.
—Adjust brightness and contrast controls to individual
and/or viewer's taste and comfort.
—Have the set at eye level—avoid looking up or down
at the picture.
—Rest occasionally by briefly looking away from the
picture—around the room or out the window.
—Wear the visual correction (glasses) prescribed for
distances beyond two feet.
—View from a distance at least five times the width of
the television screen.[10]
There is a reading problem that plagues many young
TV watchers that cannot be corrected by glasses. It is not
a physical defect. But it can be a terrible nuisance in the
classroom and affect a child's reading development. It is
called monocular, or one-eyed, vision.
Because TV conditions children to seek involvement
with the medium, kids are conditioned to seek involvement with all other media, even the print media. When
reading a book, magazine, or newspaper, they tend to
press their heads close to the printed word, as if trying to
make it a part of themselves. When a child's eyes are only
six inches from the page, it is impossible to focus both
eyes on the page, so he or she learns to read with one
eye.[11]
Television watching induces poor posture, which in
turn sets off painful physiological symptoms. That is
what Frank W. Lopez reported in the *Media Ecology
Review:* "As one British physician reported recently
before the British Royal Society of Medicine, when a

television set rests at a position lower than the person watching it, the person tilts his head downward to view the picture. This movement of the head, the doctor noted, induces a complementary slumping of the body—a kind of automatic balancing gesture—which flexes the muscles of the spine and creates a tension in them. Such is the nature of the overt adaptation system of the body. In turn, the tension in the muscles over time is translated into strain—a stiff neck, headache, and stomach disturbances are some results....''[12]

Lopez wrote about other medical findings: "The effects of induced poor posture by television watching include 'TV elbow'—caused by resting one's head in one's hand while watching television. This can cause pressure on the ulnar nerve and, depending on the length of time this is done and the person doing it, can cause numbness in the hands and arms and sometimes paralysis. Other syndromes include 'TV thrombosis'—a clotting of the veins in the legs, caused by long periods of sitting; and TV bottom!, which should be self explanatory."[13]

The purpose in revealing the potential physical health dangers in televiewing is not to motivate parents to scrap their sets or to help drive the television set makers into bankruptcy. It is to demonstrate to mothers and fathers the importance of knowing how to watch television without hurting themselves and their children. The set is a powerful collection of wires, tubes, and circuits that can hurt humans with or without pain. There have been cases of people being electrocuted while trying to fix a set themselves. Even people who know something about the guts of a set have to be cautioned when handling it. In 1971, Larry Goldstein, an editor at NBC News, was severely shocked when he tried to adjust some wires in his set. He died while being rushed to the hospital.

If parents show respect for the set's potential power to hurt a human being, the child will also. Preschoolers should *not* be allowed to tinker with a television set. In fact, parents should control channel switching, sound level, and contrast adjustment for their younger children. The preschoolers should earn the right to adjust the picture and sound. And that privilege would have to be won by demonstrating to their mother and father that they are respectful of the set's capacity to injure viewers physically. It is important also that parents insist that their children sit a safe distance from the set, nothing less than six feet away; that they watch TV no more than ninety minutes at one sitting; that there be adequate illumination in the TV viewing room.

The television set is *not* a toy.

16

Viewing Manners

Little Mark and Mary are watching *Mr. Rogers Neigh-borhood*, captivated by an experiment on transference. Their father checks his watch; he suddenly bolts out of his chair and dashes through the kitchen telling his wife, "The news is on."

When he enters the living room, he rushes past his children as if they were not in the room, cuts across their line of vision, and like an alcoholic reaching for a drink, lunges at the TV dial and switches channels.

In this home, the children don't protest because they have learned to expect such behavior from their father. They did, however, complain bitterly the first few times their father violated their TV rights and privileges. They even begged their mother to help them. But nothing could change his ways.

Certainly, the father portrayed in this episode loves his children. And if he knew how his actions around television are viewed by others, especially his children, he would become heartsick.

In too many homes, manners and courtesy, awareness of other people's feelings and needs are abandoned when a picture emerges on the TV screen. Often, adults are the worst offenders. A feeling of self-centeredness seems to sweep over them whenever they are in front of a television set. They do the kinds of things they would not want their children to do . Yet they do it, too often in full view of their children. Unfortunately, the youngsters internalize that kind of crude behavior, thinking "if Daddy and Mommy do it, it must be right."

But when kids are caught doing what they have seen their parents doing, they are usually punished, sometimes in the form of a spanking. That kind of parental reaction puzzles children, often pains them emotionally, and tragically, contributes to the building of a barrier between parent and child.

Parents should remember that their child-rearing responsibilities do not stop as soon as the set is clicked on. Most children, especially between two and seven, do most of their behavior learning at home, and their most influential models are their mothers and fathers. So it stands to reason, if parents' behavior in the television room is crude and selfish, their children will most likely adopt the same televiewing mannerisms.

Many of the indiscretions and offenses parents commit around television spring from a lack of understanding of the nature of the medium and an unawareness of the impact TV has had on themselves. The trouble is that so many of us commit indiscretions every day, unmindful of our actions and their consequences. But the child usually knows because he is the victim.

What parents must do is become more sensitive, more aware of the way they behave while watching television in a room where others, especially children, are present; they should become more understanding of their child's involvement with certain programs.

For example, if a youngster is wrapped up in a *Sesame*

Street segment and supper is ready, a parent should not holler from across the house insisting the child drop everything and come to the supper table immediately. Instead, the parent should enter the TV room and tell the child that at the end of the segment, he should turn off the set and come to supper. It is important that the parents' approach be firm—but gentle. Firm, because the child should know you mean business. Gentle, because by taking the child away from one of his favorite programs, the parent may be interfering with a genuine, enjoyable exchange with his TV friends. Imagine how a father would feel if he were absorbed in a football game on TV and his wife called him to dinner? He might utter a curse under his breath and go to the table reluctantly, feeling very sorry for himself and being uncommunicative; or he might pretend not to hear his wife's call and, after her fifth summons, demand she serve him in the TV room.

Like adults, children have feelings and a sense of justice and resent intrusion. The strong-willed children will throw temper tantrums if their TV rights are violated—a fairly common occurrence in many households today. It could just be that some children's display of anger is justified. A temper tantrum is their expression of opposition to an injustice committed against them.

Actually, parents should try to arrange meal times so they do not conflict with their children's favorite educational television shows. If, for instance, *Electric Company* runs from 5 P.M. to 5:30 P.M. in your area, and supper is usually served at 5:15, make the evening meal fifteen to twenty minutes later. The change will be worth it. The child will have been fulfilled and in a better frame of mind at the supper table than if he had been torn away from his TV friends.

Now, if for some reason a family cannot change its suppertime, it might be better, in certain cases, to keep a child from watching television for at least a half hour before supper. The reason for this is to avoid having to pull him away from something he loves. Being dragged away from a favorite TV program—one which he genuinely benefits from—could be more damaging to the child than eating cold meat and potatoes.

During a family TV-watching session, parents should be willing to answer questions which do not take long to explain. Lengthy explanations, however, could disrupt the rest of the family's viewing of a program that the parents carefully selected because of its cultural, educational, or wholesome entertainment value. On the other hand, the child's inquiry should be addressed. The best time to answer is during a commercial break or immediately after the show. When a complicated question is asked by a child, the parent should tell the youngster in a sympathetic but firm manner that he will have to wait. It may be a strain, but a parent who promises to answer a child's question should fulfill that promise. Obviously, to do this requires remembering the questions. Neglecting to answer them could cause the child to challenge his parent's credibility and lose respect for him.

Should a parent not know the answer to a child's question, the parent should suggest looking it up in the encyclopedia or some other source with the child. Doing this could help tighten the child-parent bond and impress upon the little one the importance of books.

By limiting questioning during a family television session, and explaining the reason for the restriction, parents teach children to respect and appreciate the rights of others and to become more sensitive to other people's feelings.

While it is important that children learn not to interrupt family televiewing, it is equally important that parents learn to avoid verbally abusing children around the set.

This means being patient and understanding and never angrily "shushing" a child as you would a frisky dog. A child is a human being. He should be addressed in the language he understands and in a compassionate tone of voice. After all, the questions a child asks are meaningful to him. The manner in which a parent addresses a child's question communicates to the tot the degree of his parent's interest in him. Most children will accept waiting for an answer until the end of a show without feeling hurt or neglected if the parent's initial response is sympathetic. Too often parents who are wrapped up in a TV show will recoil harshly at a questioning youngster. That kind of reaction damages the child-parent relationship and psychologically wounds the youngster.

When a parent is watching a children's program only with a child, the restriction on questions should be loosened. How much depends largely on the questioning and the responses. If it is lively, and the child seems to be gaining educationally from the exchange, the parent should feel no guilt if he and the child miss the remainder of the program. In such a case, TV would have acted as a stimulant to a more fruitful experience for both child and parent. During the discussion, it is conceivable that the two could pore through literature together, trying to find the answers to the questions the child raised. In most cases, such a discussion would end up being a healthy parent-child interaction, an occurrence too few parents and children experience today.

One crucial point: during the discussion, the parent should not turn off the set. Doing that would distract the youngster, break the atmospheric spell and end the discussion. Let the set play. It is the child's Muzak. It is strange, but many children who turn their backs on the TV and play with their friends or toys seem connected to what's on television and will respond actively and usually indignantly should someone turn off the set or even switch channels. I am sure many parents have experienced this phenomenon.

There are times when a child watching TV alone will call to his mother who is in another room and ask her a question relating to the program. Parents should not make a habit of yelling answers back. If this is done repeatedly, the child will learn to respond the same way under similar conditions. There will be times, however, when the only parental response needed is a shout. This would be acceptable, for example, whenever a child wants to know his parents' whereabouts. But the shout should not be tinged with anger—just a loud comforting yell.

Most parental responses should be determined by the urgency of the child's request and what the parent is doing at the time of the call. In most cases, the best approach is to go to the child and answer his question face to face. It might turn into another stimulating, heart-to-heart discussion. On the other hand, parents should not allow themselves to become their children's slaves. Children must understand that parents, like themselves, have needs and rights also. They must understand too that there will be times when a parent simply cannot comply with their wish. They must learn to accept that condition without whimpering or fussing. The danger in always responding positively to a child's call from a TV room is spoiling him. In too many homes, a youngster's call sets off an instantaneous reaction in the parent: the parent drops everything he or she is doing, races to the dear one to do his bidding immediately, which could mean getting the child a peeled banana or a bowl full of bubbles before the commercial ends.

17

Parents!
Schools Can't Deal
with TV-Watching Kids

Children love television, and because they love it, they learn from it. Preschoolers singing TV jingles while playing is evidence of that. So is that new challenge to elementary school educators: the counting and reading five-year-old, the graduates of PBS's children's programming.

Many elementary school teachers who take *Sesame Street, Mister Rogers Neighborhood* or *Electric Company* seriously develop an inferiority complex.

"How can I compete?" they wonder—often painfully. An understandable question which pushes some into professional paralysis.

Pretending that these outstanding children's television programs don't exist won't help. That type of escapism either creates a teacher-student communications gap or widens an existing one. After all, the kids will continue to watch, and will continue to measure, consciously or unconsciously, their teacher's performance with those of Bill Cosby, Loretta Long (she's *Sesame Street's* Susan), or Fred Rogers. TV programs like *Electric Company* won't vanish. In fact, we can expect more

163

of them, most likely better executed and more appealing to children, thus aggravating the teacher's worry about TV threatening her job security.

Though most teachers don't have the training to be TV performers, they are performers nevertheless. Instead of gazing into camera lenses, they peer daily into children's eyes. Admittedly, the classroom audience is a tough one, kids' attention span is usually short, their interests are varied and underdeveloped, and their bias against school sprouts on sunny days.

Too many children sit in classrooms in body only, thinking technicolor thoughts of distant lands and beyond, where *Star Trek* circulates, of the moon, where astronauts pick for clues, and of being back home, embraced by television beams.

Through that box with the big tube, boys and girls have visited stone-age villages in New Guinea, Moscow circuses, China's Great Wall; they've explored ocean floors and climbed mountain peaks; they have witnessed wars fought and adults arguing. They have learned from television, commercial as well as public, without being tested, graded, or reprimanded by a teacher.

No doubt about it, competition from TV is real, but teachers must learn to use the medium as a positive force, helping children grow in mind and spirit. To resist television as a factor in the educational development of a child is to view him with blurred vision, to listen to him from afar, to deny a major intellectual and personality-shaping force in his life. That kind of blindness in a teacher is usually sensed by a child as rejection of him. When that happens in the classroom, the teacher fails.

Perhaps a child's most impressionable stage in his personality development is between ages of three to five. It is during this critical period in his life that a child who is at home spends nearly 64 percent of his waking hours watching TV.[1]

It is also estimated that only sleep surpasses television as the top time consumer for American school children. Teachers should also know that during an average year, the older child attends school 980 hours and watches TV 1,340 hours, so that by the time he graduates from high school, he will have spent roughly 11,000 hours in the classroom and more than 22,000 hours in front of the television set.[2]

Obviously that much time devoted to TV watching has to have some impact on a human being, especially a young one who is less suspicious, more open, more vulnerable to TV's messages than the adult. The power of TV's influence on children was demonstrated to a young University of Massachusetts doctoral candidate three years ago while in the army in Vietnam. During a Vietcong attack, he reported in class, mortars started exploding around his bunker and at first it all seemed like another TV show to him. Later, he found himself scrapping what he learned in basic infantry training and resorting to fighting techniques he learned watching dramatized battle scenes on TV. This was a case of a young soldier trusting TV more than his drill sergeant. But one doesn't have to wait nineteen years before noticing what impact TV has on young people. We have spotted how it affects even those in diapers.

Three years ago, the mother of a fourteen-month-old girl told the executive producer of *Sesame Street* that her daughter can identify by name all the *Sesame Street* people—the four live regulars on the show, Gordon, Susan, Bob, and Mr. Hooper, the muppets—and can recite the ABCs and her numbers.[3] There are literally thousands of similar stories that have reached Children's

Television Workshop. And many more that are circulated between families, passed on during coffee breaks or while playing bridge.

Back in the 1930s—the pre-TV era—preschoolers rarely displayed the kind of highly developed observational powers of the TV-age child. Nor were they so aware of the exploits, the household procedures, even the intrigues of the adult world. Thirty years ago most children were awed by adults. Through TV, today's children see how adults live, work, and play, and many of them are not impressed with what they see. In fact, many have lost respect for the adults and have even developed a superior attitude toward older people, including their parents. That attitude is carried to school. In most instances the teacher, especially if he's practicing pre-TV educational methods, is viewed by many kids as a tyrant, a fool, or simply a figure empowered and programmed to control thirty hours a week of a student's life—nothing else! Which category students place their teacher in depends, in large measure, on the teacher's personality.

Children exposed to television since infancy know more, are more worldly, than America's children of twenty-five years ago. Because they love and trust television, they have internalized much of what they have watched, which has made them into little adults who are often insulted by teachers who treat them like the children of the 1930s. Many teachers make the mistake of drawing upon their own childhood experiences to reach today's child. The mistake is assuming that her feelings, her behavior, her view of the world as a child is the same as her student's. In the 1930s and 40s, when some teachers were in grade school, there were no communications satellites and there was no live TV coverage of voyages to the moon or the Olympic games in Japan. Nor were there televised assassinations of famous figures;

and *Sesame Street, Electric Company,* and *Mister Rogers Neighborhood* were not even in the dream stage of development; and most importantly, there was no instrument around like the TV set that seduces its users into becoming its faithful lover.

Today's teacher who is thirty or older was confined to a child's world during his elementary-school years, and he seemed to know his place. He viewed the world through fantasy media like comic books, the funny pages, movie serials, and radio programs—all entertaining experiences but not very believable. He learned by "hitting the books" and succeeded professionally by becoming a skillful practitioner of an educational process designed to punch out productive producers of things. He believed the position of his country in the world was due, in large measure, to the soundness of its educational systems which produced him—and that he now proudly serves.

The younger teacher, about twenty-five, though exposed to TV most of his or her life discovered that he had to negate, at least consciously, television's impact on him to make way for early childhood education views of professors who were either ignorant of TV's influence on children or who simply detested TV and refused to accept its reality. He graduated filled with information about educational methods and classroom decorum designed for turn-of-the-century children, somewhat confused and unprepared to really serve the children of the TV generation in which he could legitimately claim membership.

Actually, the educational setting in most schools is out of focus. Teachers and students are on different communications wave lengths. Let's face it, TV has contributed to this communications breakdown, and many teachers—people who care about children and education—are at a loss as to how to reach their students meaningfully.

One way is for teachers, educational administrators, and educational theorists and dreamers to recognize TV's existence and power, to understand its impact on people, especially the young who have been deeply influenced by television, and that means the great majority of children who go to school today.

For educators to ignore what television is doing to the human beings they are charged with educating is like farmers rejecting the influence of water and sunlight on their crops.

Observing how children act while watching TV could make teachers more effective classroom communicators. By spotting what captures children's attention and noticing what bores them, teachers could develop new ways of making school an exciting place to be.

Instead of cursing television as an antieducational and corrupting force, teachers should view it as an ally, using it as a learning and enrichment experience for their students. After all, doesn't a successful teacher employ those communications skills and vehicles that can best reach and stimulate students? Why not TV, something children love?

Teachers should learn to appreciate how TV shapes their students' view of themselves, of their friends, of school, and of the world in general. But most importantly, teachers should discover how TV has conditioned their students for formal education. Having been nurtured on TV since infancy, today's child is a picture- and image-oriented student who sits in a classroom being taught by a word-oriented teacher. To appreciate, to understand what has influenced the students she is teaching, the teacher should watch the TV programs her children are most likely watching. They should be viewed with an unbiased eye and, if possible, in a child's state of mind. Seems silly, I know, but it is a way of developing some idea, some feeling for what children enjoy and respect. It usually follows that what children enjoy they internalize. Viewing children's TV could provide the teacher with an opportunity of understanding her students' view of their world. That kind of insight could inspire her to scrap outmoded educational approaches for those tailored to reach and excite the child of the TV generation. And, if there are none available, she might dare to create some.

If she doesn't she will be overwhelmed when she tries to cope with the legions of *Sesame Street* graduates who enter school knowing numbers and letters far better than their predecessors did. Unfortunately, teachers aren't being trained to deal with the television-influenced child, nor are school administrators providing their teachers with such training—or new curriculum. As Professor Harold Shane of Indiana University puts it: "There is virtually no planning of curriculum change underway at the elementary school level that anticipates the needs of children who will bring to the primary school two, three, and even four years of carefully designed experience."[4]

However, there are a few educators who are doing some serious thinking about the problem. Ronald E. Sutton, executive secretary of the National Association of Media Educators, has some sound practical advice. "An intelligent discussion of yesterday's *Lucy* show can serve both to correct the misapprehensions about American life it has left in young minds and provide a springboard for more valid insights. *Star Trek* might do the same for a science class; *Dragnet* for a study of law; the news coverage of Watergate for a better understanding of all of the strengths and weaknesses of our most fundamental institutions."[5]

18

Controlling TV Watching in the Home

There are close to 90 million television sets in the United States, being used on the average more than seven hours a day. More than two-thirds of those sets are in homes where children live.[1] Tragically, very little control is being exercised in these homes, even in many homes where parents carefully choose their children's experiences. These parents act as if watching television is no experience at all.

Researchers at Columbia University discovered that as few as 5 percent of families control TV viewing, and even those families limit control to the amount of watching, ignoring the content of what is watched.[2]

Understandably, there are reasons for this condition: Some parents like to use television as a baby-sitter and pacifier and do not want to upset the tranquility of their home environment; many are unaware of the psychological and physiological harm excessive TV watching can cause in humans; there are the permissive parents who philosophically consider their children as equals to adults and refuse to interfere with their tot's efforts to chart his own destiny; and then there is the American laissez-faire tradition, in which control is equated with the suppression of freedom.

That is a lot to overcome. But unless parents take direct action in controlling TV watching in the home, they will continue to subject their children to a behavior-shaping medium which could warp their outlook of life and twist their personalities. There is a strong chance of that happening, even though psychologists differ on how much influence TV has in molding human behavior. Very little research has been done in this area, but much of what has been done by such eminently qualified scientists as Dr. Albert Bandura, Dr. Robert Leibert, Dr. James Bryun, Dr. Joseph Dominick, and Dr. Bradley Greenberg shows a correlation between children's TV watching and the development of their behavior.

Parents should control their children's TV watching for the same reason they should restrain them from playing in a street with heavy traffic. In a sense, parents should act as traffic lights in homes where TV exists and employ that function until their children are disciplined enough to be their own traffic lights.

In controlling TV watching, it is important to avoid being repressive or primitive, for that could dull a child's spirit and force him into a behavioral mold into which he does not naturally fit. That kind of approach would alienate kids and seriously strain parent-child relationships.

Parents must take into account the reality and permanence of television in our society and its natural pull on children. They should protect them from what is bad on TV, help to sift through television's offerings for what would enrich them, help them grow happier and healthier, and assure them that watching TV purely for entertainment's sake will not be eliminated.

If handled with sensitivity, children will accept their parents' effort to control home televiewing as a genuine manifestation of their love for them. After all, it takes extra time and considerable energy. If parents didn't care about their children, they wouldn't take on another heavy responsibility. The easy way out would be to do nothing, allowing their children to feed their TV habit.

Granted, finding the time to generate the patience, the energy, and strength to control the home television situation may seem too taxing to today's busy parents. But parents must either meet this challenge or allow their children to continue to be psychologically scorched by unabated television viewing. If parents love their children, they'll find the time.

Wresting control of TV away from children is a sensitive undertaking, especially in the home where kids have never been blocked from turning on the set. Above all, parents should avoid becoming a barrier between TV and their children. If they do, they stand the risk of turning into an enemy of their children. Many of these youngsters have developed a strong attachment to television; some have even become addicted to it. Springing television restrictions on them without warning could alienate the young TV lovers, causing some to dislike, even hate, their mother and father. Setting off such an inflammatory emotional reaction is understandable, because TV is the primary source of pleasure to many children. It takes them places their parents can't afford to take them; it pays attention to them when they're lonely—and as far as they are concerned it never punishes. Many children grow to love, to believe, TV and consider it their trusted friend. A hasty, harsh handling of the home TV situation could be interpreted by a child as parental rejection of his best friend.

In breaking a child's TV-viewing habits, be gentle, be patient, for it is like weaning a child from a security blanket. You don't suddenly pounce on a child's blanket and yank it away forever.

When both parents are clear as to why they should control family TV watching, they should consult together as to what form it should take, how it should be implemented and managed. Both parents must support each other's decisions and try not to compromise the standards they have drawn up.

In devising standards, parents should consider the degree of dependency each child has on TV, the amount of time each child should watch TV daily, the kinds of programs children should be prohibited from watching, the types of shows they should be encouraged to watch. They should also take into account the different personalities and natures of the children involved. All of this is important to consider, because some children have developed a greater need for TV and have a deeper attachment to it than others. Why subject a child who only watches TV an hour a day to the approach required to unhook a TV addict? Dealing with the addict will require more parental attention, more parental control, more parental imagination in weaning him from the set.

While the approach in dealing with each child should be different, all of the children should abide by a uniform set of television viewing standards something like this:

TV Watching Standards for Children

1. Time limit for TV watching: preschoolers: no more than ninety minutes a day; seven to ten years: no more than two hours a day; ten to twelve years: no more than two hours and thirty minutes a day. It is important that the children's TV watching be fragmented, never

longer that ninety minutes at one sitting. Excessive TV viewing does cause fatigue in some children.

2. When you are doubtful about the worth of a program and have no way of finding out about its content, do not gamble: Keep your children from seeing it. Substitute another activity for the time allotted to televiewing.

3. Children should *not* be allowed to turn on the TV without parental permission.

4. Programs that feature violence for violence' sake should *not* be viewed by children. Some examples: Most of the detective series, westerns, and war episodes. Violence on documentaries or news shows or historical episodes are okay, simply because it is an actual portrayal of life. Here, parents should be with their children, ready to observe their reactions and explain the reason for the violent act.

5. Prohibit programs that reinforce racism or ethnic prejudices and stereotypes. Do not let little children, especially preschoolers, watch programs like *All in the Family,* or *Laugh-in* simply because young children take everything at face value; they have no appreciation for satire or puns. Besides, these programs demonstrate violence through dialogue and facial expressions (they can teach kids how to tear people apart with the tongue). These programs model backbiting extremely well.

6. Avoid family situation shows that provide unrealistic home settings that could frustrate a child, causing him to prefer TV families over his own, to hate his living conditions, even his parents.

7. Try to keep children from viewing TV commercials. One way to do this is have children watch PBS programs as much as possible. When watching commercial TV, use a special push-button gadget to black out commercials. The gadget is available in most shops that sell TV sets.

8. No TV watching after supper during a school day unless something extraordinary is to be aired, at which time the whole family should try to watch together. What constitutes "extraordinary"? Something culturally rewarding, educational, exceptionally newsworthy. For example, a moonshot launching, a film like *Raisin in the Sun* or a Christmas special like *Amahl and the Night Visitors*.

Parents should devise standards for themselves as well—and try to abide by them. Certainly their standards are going to be different from their children's, but the kids would understand the reason for the difference. They have already learned through other experiences that adults have more cultivated tastes, more mature interests.

By setting standards for themselves, parents communicate to their children that they really believe what they say, but more importantly, that they feel so strongly about the need to control television use in the home that they are willing to restrict their own TV watching, even though they may find TV viewing extremely enjoyable. By adhering to these standards, parents also have an opportunity to model integrity.

The consequences of parents' ignoring the standards they set for themselves could be painful, even heartbreaking. It could establish a gap between what is said and what is done—something children have an uncanny knack for noticing and pointing out. Or children might stamp their parents as hypocrites without telling them, causing a continually widening communications gap, a gap that is never addressed by either side but which leads to deeper estrangement, even hostility, between children and parents.

The late psychologist Dr. Haim G. Ginott provided some guidance on how parents should approach the subject of television controls with their children: "Limits should be phrased in a language that does not challenge the child's self-respect. Limits are heeded better when stated succinctly and impersonally.

" 'No movies on school nights' arouses less resentment than 'You know you can't go to the movie on school nights.'

" 'It's bed time' is more readily accepted than 'You are too young to stay up that late.' "[3]

Discussions about TV should not turn into heated arguments. The fury and anger of an argument clouds intended messages and could set off hostility between parent and child or intensify existing hostilities between them. Also, parents should avoid preaching, for that could force a child to withdraw in spirit or become defensive. They should level with their children and express themselves with sincerity. If they do that, the chances are that their children will react positively.

Parents should not "bad mouth" television, for if children then spot their mother and father watching TV they will lose respect for them. Kids reason: "If you watch it, you must like it."

When talking to children about TV, parents should be positive in their attitude and fair in their judgment, acknowledging the good and bad.

Children should be encouraged to ask questions, to inquire where they could secure more information about something they have seen on TV that fascinated them. And, parents should try to help their kids find the right sources. That kind of aid could demonstrate to kids the value of books.

All of the children should have access to the *TV Guide* or the newspaper's TV section. If there is a program they wish to watch, they should bring it up and be prepared to give reasons why they should be allowed to watch the program.

Older children should be allowed to view more TV than their younger brothers and sisters and, depending upon their age, should be allowed to see shows with more mature themes. For example, teenagers should be allowed to see movies like *Jane Eyre* or *A Streetcar Named Desire*, even *The Longest Day*.

Controlling TV is a sensitive responsibility. Parents must anticipate infractions of the home's TV standards, especially shortly after they are introduced. You can't expect kids to change their televiewing ways immediately. There are going to be slips. How infractions are handled is crucial. Most often infractions are simply the result of forgetfulness. So parents must guard against challenging their child's self-respect or hurting his feelings. A parent should address the child's action in a gentle but firm manner and never attack the person. "You probably forgot about watching shows like that" is more readily accepted by children than "You know you are not supposed to see shows like that. Turn it off."

If a seven-year-old is found watching more than two hours of TV, parents shouldn't pounce on the child as if he were a criminal. Again, they should address the action and remind the child of the standard that has been violated: "Time is up for TV today. Remember, two hours a day of television."

Hopefully, after a few months the children would be so conditioned to the TV controls that they would have internalized them.

Because of excessive TV watching, more and more families rarely meet and consult as a unit. Family unity suffers. In some households members of a family may never utter a word to each other for days, because most of their free time is spent communicating with the characters on the TV screen. They move through the house as strangers. Or if there is verbal communication it may be in the form of an incomplete sentence, sounding like a semigroan or grunt. Why, in many homes during prime-time evening TV, the refrigerator receives more attention than human beings!

But this damaging situation need not exist. In fact, television could be a means of helping to restore or strengthen family cohesion. One way is for the family to watch TV together. In many American homes all the members of a family watch TV in the same room. But rarely do they watch as a family. In reality, they watch as a group of individuals, oblivious to other people's feelings in the room, exchanging words only if someone's foot or elbow is blocking the TV tube.

Snoring and the munching of potato chips or pretzels are about the only other human sounds heard during a TV-viewing session in many homes. And the longest, most spirited dialogue occurs when a decision has to be made as to what show will be seen next.

Parents should make a special effort to point out which programs they would like to have the family watch together. By watching with their children, parents demonstrate to them that they do not consider TV an enemy but, more important, that they want to be with their children, sharing the same pastime. That simple act can draw a parent and child closer together, especially if they interact while watching.

There are ways to stimulate interest in the programs you choose. When my wife and I, for example, discovered that *Elizabeth R*—that splendid British TV series that was shown on the Public Broadcasting Service network during the winter of 1971—was to be featured on a local commercial television station, we chose to watch the series as a family. Our five-year-old was excluded because of the hour it was to be shown; and besides, the series was a bit too mature for her.

To motivate interest in *Elizabeth R*, we mentioned to our eleven, twelve, and sixteen-year-old sons that a unique production technique was used to produce the series and explained what it was. I pointed out why Elizabeth was a great monarch and tried to paint a word picture of life in Britain during her reign, underscoring her triumphs, failures, conflicts, and intrigues, the areas most children find exciting in the programs they normally watch. The fact that an Emmy winner was playing the role of Elizabeth R was also mentioned.

The *TV Guide* blurb on *Elizabeth R* and the reference to her in the encyclopedia supplied us with information we needed to stimulate our boys to want to watch the series. After the first program, it did not take any more effort on our parts to arouse their interest in *Elizabeth R*. The program became the motivator.

Our boys benefited from this experience in a number of ways: It was an absorbing history lesson, excellent drama; they were exposed to powerful, witty writing and outstanding acting. And it was good entertainment.

Elizabeth R became a topic of conversation around our dinner table. The program also inspired our boys to dig into the encyclopedia to find out more about the dynamic, colorful, proud lady who ruled Britain for forty-five years in the sixteenth century.

Of course, we enjoyed the company of our sons while watching *Elizabeth R* and they enjoyed having us with them, sharing a beautiful art experience.

Watching TV together as a family should not be viewed as a surrender to an appealing popular media fad, but rather a recognition of the reality of TV, its deep-rooted position in society, its influence in almost every phase of human life. TV is pregnant with humanity-helping potentialities. It challenges both society and the individual. Society must learn to harness this electronic force and channel it for constructive uses; the individual, on the other hand, must rise above TV's tendency to control and dominate lives and learn to use it to help himself grow culturally and intellectually.

Television is no enemy of humankind, no mass-media Satan that's driven to numb the minds of men, leaving humanity blobbish and spiritless. Yet there are people who act as if TV is their enemy—and refuse to buy a set or even glance at one that is on. Some intensely passionate TV haters react violently to TV when it is mentioned—even in front of their children. Of course, the kids know TV exists and if given the opportunity will sneak away from their house to watch television in their friends' homes or elsewhere.

For twentieth-century man to reject TV because it can hurt people is like rejecting the airplane because airplanes can be used as bombers. Instead of rejecting and cursing television, the parent who detests TV should accept it, at least for the sake of his child. He must resolve to control it and devise ways of operationalizing the controls.

Many TV haters are really secret TV lovers; they avoid television because they know they can easily be seduced by it and caused to waste precious time. If for some reason a TV-hating parent can't control TV for himself, he should still make TV available for his children. To deny children good television is to bar them from experiences which could broaden their outlook on life, but more importantly could cut them off from an aspect of reality that society accepts. A hermit or monk could deal with this kind of media denial. And rural families with strong interpersonal bonds could, I'm sure, live a healthy, happy life without TV. For they can use the forest, the mountains, the streams, the lakes, as their playground. Instead of watching television, rural families can go hiking, skating, fishing, and mountain climbing, and observe how beavers build dams. But most Americans don't live in the country any more. In fact, the great majority of people live in the cities or suburbs. When an urban or suburban parent bans TV viewing in his home, he stands the risk of producing children who interact awkwardly with other children in the neighborhood.

American children, especially between the ages of three to ten, consume heaps of TV. Why, it is estimated that the average three- to five-year-old child watches fifty-four hours of TV a week. That kind of exposure is bound to influence a child's play habits. Many urban children, playing in the street, in the yard, or in the park are often involved in games centered around their favorite TV programs, and their conversations are riddled with catchy sayings of popular TV characters such as Popeye, *Sesame Street's* Cookie Monster, and Freddie Flintstone.

A youngster unfamiliar with TV's fare could find making friends or breaking into the neighborhood gang a strain. He could also become the block's "oddball."

A case in point: An intern teacher working with first graders revealed to me how a little girl was ostracized by four of her classmates because her parents would not allow her to watch television. One afternoon the teacher overheard a conversation in the playground involving five girls. Four of them were berating the other one for not knowing what the Cookie Monster had said the day before on *Sesame Street*. The four girls took turns imitating the Cookie Monster, leaving the youngster who doesn't have TV alone, feeling rejected by girls she would like to be friends with.

This is not an isolated case. It happens too often, unfortunately, never reaching the ear of a parent or teacher. Only the child—the target of the ridicule—knows.

I raise this point not to push parents to accept blindly popular social practices like televiewing because acceptance of TV would guarantee their children a wholesome relationship with the nieghborhood children. TV is no magic that can assure such a relationship. It is, however, important for anti-TV parents to be aware of how their extreme media position could affect their children outside of the home, and that it is unfair to project their own prejudices upon their children.

Parents who are trying to control television viewing could use more help from their local newspaper or periodicals like *TV Guide* or *Parents'* magazine. The print media should be able to provide parents with more information concerning the merit of programs in relation to children. Certainly a successful magazine like *TV Guide* could establish a responsible and fair way of measuring the safety and educational worth of children's programs. One way would be to set up a board made up of early childhood specialists, child psychologists, pediatricians, and deeply concerned parents. This board would review programs, citing the advantages and disadvantages of a child's seeing them. A special code could be developed which would give parents a good idea of whether to allow their children to see a program or not. A code symbol could be placed beside the title of the program. The magazine could also list the programs they recommend for children and make it available to all newspapers in the country.

Of course, an even better idea would be for *TV Guide* or some other magazine to establish a separate weekly TV-listing periodical, dealing only with children's programming. The magazine would also run features on how parents could use existing programs more effectively in the home—for example, an article that isolates the teaching techniques of *Sesame Street* and shows parents how to use those techniques in a home setting.

Many of the suggestions I offer in this chapter are simply that—suggestions. Many parents may want to devise their own methods of controlling television suited to their family's particular life style and needs. However, what is important is that every family institute some controls. Certainly, the previous chapters give reasons why this is necessary.

19

Portrait of the
First TV Generation

America's first TV generation is living—and the rest of
the nation is aware of their presence, for they have been
very visible, vocal, and different. They are the people
between the ages of seventeen and twenty-seven who
always knew TV, knew it as well as or even better than
most of their relatives. It sustained them during unhappy
periods and lonely days, filling the voids in their lives.

Their daily exposure to television throughout their
lives helped to make these people what they are today.
Their TV experiences have been internalized. A careful
analysis of the TV programming content and style and
commercials over the past twenty-five years should give
a psychologist a fairly good attitudinal, character, and
personality profile of a member of the first TV-age generation. In other words, most seventeen- to twenty-seven-
year-old Americans are, at least partially, a composite
reflection of what they have been exposed to on TV
during their lifetime.

A TV-generation human being is not cast in a certain
appearance mold. His uniform is not long hair, a beard,
beads, and sandals, although there are probably many

people who subscribe to that mode of fashion who belong to the TV generation. The same is true of the dress and brassiere-wearing young lady. Belonging to the TV generation has to do with attitude, outlook, mannerisms, a way of living.

Television produced a people with a view of the world that no other American generation ever experienced, making them into a people whose behavior challenged our national mores, buried Victorianism, and made their parents embarrassed, bewildered, and, at times, angry.

They dare to express their disenchantment with existing values and, unlike most previous youth generations, are creating and experimenting with new value systems and adopting new outlooks which their elders find difficult to grasp. They are people, by and large, with a global consciousness, who do not get goose bumps when they see a parade on July Fourth. They are Earthlings first and Americans second, even though most of them may not be able to articulate this consciousness.

Most of their parents don't share this view. They are more rooted to the home and their community and pay allegiance to the flag because they have been conditioned to do so at home, at school, and at church. And when their children look beyond their immediate surroundings for stimulation and knowledge the parents question their patriotism and gratefulness to their country. What happens is, the parents project their own feelings and concepts onto their children, whom they have allowed to watch TV all of their lives. This privilege, of course, was a pleasure that transported them away from their home, school, and church every day of their lives, taking them to jungles, South Pacific islands, and the Arctic, to Egyptian pyramids, Mayan ruins, and the Cathedral of Notre Dame, to the police station, to Congress, to the United Nations, to the ocean floor and to the moon, to the hospital to witness the birth of a human being and to watch death snare a man. By giving their children free rein of the TV set, parents inadvertently contributed to their children's different outlook of life.

When kids saw our planet Earth on TV, blue and white and beautiful, as seen from a rocket ship thousands of miles in space, they believed what they saw. But though many of their parents accepted what they saw intellectually, they had some unexplainable emotional reservations. These doubts are quite understandable when you consider that most parents were brought up feeling that the center of the world was their community, that outer space is for the likes of former comic-strip characters Flash Gordon and Buck Rogers.

Because of their global consciousness, the TV-generation people show deep concern for the plight of people in different areas of the world. They were moved by the pain of the Vietnamese. Their concern became so intense that many of them dared to challenge their government and shake their fists in its face, whereas most of the older generation maintained a rather detached attitude toward the suffering of a people who looked and spoke differently from their neighbors.

Those belonging to the TV generation have shown a readiness to help the socially and economically deprived, and seem to have a greater social consciousness than their parents. Many of them are entering social work and volunteering for the Peace Corps and Vista. In universities, more students than ever before are studying the behavioral sciences because they want to be equipped to help others and they want to know more about how humans function. Sociology is popular because students want to know how to improve the quality of life in our society. And there seems to be a greater yearning for spiritual development among some of these people because of a desire to become better human beings. Better human beings, they feel, will make more harmonious communities.

In a way, the TV-generation people feel that the Earth is their country, that all of the people on it belong to the same family: the Family of Man. Their parents, on the other hand, don't share that belief. In fact, they agonize over why their children spend so much energy and time working for projects and causes outside the home and community. Down deep they view their children as traitors, for they believe their children's first allegiance should be to their family. Of course, the TV-generation people agree. The only trouble is—they have a different concept of familyhood.

Because the TV-generation people grew up with television, they understand the medium a lot better than their parents. Their knowledge of it is intuitive. TV is a part of them, having seeped into their consciousness as if through osmosis, practically since infancy. They seem to understand TV's nature, and because of this many of them understand its power. And some, like the Yippies, a radical segment of the TV-generation population, use TV as a weapon of attack against their enemies. Jerry Rubin, the Yippie leader, writes about it in his book *Do It!* Rubin's description of how to use television effectively shows an innate feeling for the medium: "Television is a nonverbal instrument! The way to understand TV is to shut off the sound. No one remembers any words they hear; the mind is a technicolor movie of images, not words."

"I've never seen 'bad' coverage of a demonstration. It makes no difference what they [TV] say about us. The pictures are the story."

Rubin and his followers understand TV's ability to brainwash and wish that their organization possessed control of television: "If the Yippies controlled TV, we could make the Viet Cong and the Black Panthers the heroes of swooning American middle-aged housewives everywhere within a week."

But Rubin and his people have had some success with television without operating the TV industry. Having a feel for TV, they know how to manipulate it; they know what and how to exploit what is shown on TV: "Walter Cronkite is SDS's best organizer. Uncle Walter brings out the map of the U.S. with circles around the campuses that blew up today."

He then points out how a news report like that affects the TV-age kid who is watching: "Every kid out there is thinking, 'Wow! I wanna see my campus on that map!' Television proves the domino theory: a campus falls and they all fall. The first 'student demonstration' flashed across the TV tubes of the nation as a myth in 1964. That year the first generation being raised from birth on TV was 9, 10, and 11 years old. 'First chance I get,' they thought, 'I wanna do that too.' The first chance they got was when they got to junior high and high school five years later—1969! And that was the year America's junior high and high schools exploded! A government survey shows that three out of every five high schools in the country had 'some form of active protest' in 1969.

"TV is raising generations of kids who want to grow up and become demonstrators.

"Have you ever seen boring demonstrations on TV? Just being on TV makes it exciting. Even picket lines look breathtaking. Television creates myths bigger than reality.

"Demonstrations last hours, and most of the time nothing happens. After the demonstration we rush home for the six o'clock news. The drama review. TV packs all the action into two minutes—a commercial for the revolution."[1]

The Yippie leader views TV as a necessary weapon in any modern revolutionary's arsenal.

Since Rubin's book was published, the television networks and local TV news departments have grown more restrained in covering demonstrations. They now understand the effect some of their zealous enterprise can have on the TV-age young man and woman. Their thinking now is: "When there are fewer demonstrations on TV, there are going to be fewer demonstrations on campuses."

The TV-generation person is an agent for social change yet he is unaware of functioning in such a role. Because he sees so much of the world, he sees lots of its flaws, which he feels should be corrected. So even if he doesn't join a change-oriented organization, he may champion a change-oriented cause, openly or quietly. Just by believing in the need for social change, the quiet believer helps to weave an atmosphere of receptivity to change and the cause. He helps to keep the need for change and the cause "in the air."

Among the things the TV-generation people see that pre-television age youth didn't see is the way adults behave toward each other and operate professionally. TV provides them with a microscopic view. The exposure has affected the young viewers differently, creating two extreme reactions. For one group the hypocrisy, deception, and dishonesty have had a profound effect on them. Some have been so repulsed by what they have seen all of their lives on TV that they have rejected the established social system and say what comes into mind and heart—swear words and all. These people abhor pretense and worship naturalness. They "tell it like it is," find out what they really want to do, and then "do their thing." Others, however, are less sensitive, and have adopted the adult behavior they have seen on TV. Because they have seen so much of it, it has been drilled into them. They have become master maneuverers of the "system," more adroit than their parents in "wheeling and dealing," more ruthless in their drive to achieve business objectives.

Which category a TV-generation person falls into depends, in large measure, on the person's upbringing, the quality and quantity of parental guidance he has experienced, the kinds of TV programming and commercials he has watched and, of course, his nature.

They are a people who tend to think in pictures and images, who express themselves better through drawing, painting, dance, photography, and music than through writing. Many of them are poor spellers and have difficulty making themselves understood on paper and orally. They are a people who use their hands and the rest of their body to express themselves a lot more than those in past American generations.

Some of them have been so saturated with television, they find books as awkward to handle as literate people find ancient hieroglyphics.

They are an impatient people. Mainly because TV has conditioned them to expect quick solutions to individual and societal problems.

Their impatience, their quest for naturalness, their directness, their distaste for compromise makes them a simplistic people. Actually, they are easier to understand, because they have no hidden agendas and tend to be above-board.

Because many of them have given up on our system, they feel *no* real allegiance to any tradition, they tend to be more willing to experiment with new modes of living, explore new ideas, and try new means of stimulation.

They like traveling. And money does not seem to be an obstacle to taking trips, because for them the thumb is as effective as a bus or train ticket. But their lust for travel is also a desire to escape, a desire conditioned by the thousands of hours of escape before the TV set. Their preoccupation with escape made them ripe candidates for drugs. They actually became the vanguard of the drug culture.

They have deep feelings about preserving the physical beauty of our planet and preventing people from pillaging it.

They are more tolerant of differences than their parents; however, their tolerance is more nihilistic than altruistic and "do your thing" is a motto they have coined and live by. Sex is talked about openly and practiced with less anguish and guilt. Daily exposure to commercials and programs that stress the importance and pleasure of sexual triumph has helped to make them sexually freer. In fact, to them sexual intercourse is as common as necking was to their parents when they were single. Marriage is considered more of a process than a duty and couples will test their relationship before marriage by living together to see if they truly belong together. Legalizing a deep male and female relationship doesn't have the solemn impact that such an experience had on their parents. Therefore they don't feel as obligated to stick with a spouse if the process of marriage becomes painful and sticky. And with some the marriage ritual is considered a charade and they never bother signing any documents, paying any fees, or saying "I do."

Many TV-generation men and women approve of the woman's struggle for emancipation. They are willing to break sexist traditions, so that both sexes share chores equally and compete equally for the same jobs. The men are not ashamed to wash dishes, change diapers, or vacuum the living room. Women drive taxis and planes and dare to aspire to professional and social heights their mothers never dreamed of.

Violence, human suffering, bloodshed, and war are as natural to them as a mother's breast is to an infant. They have seen it all on TV—and it has hurt them, making them insecure, fearful, and anxious. But they manifest their insecurity in different ways. Some wonder when and where the next war will break out, whether they will have to take up arms and kill. They lean toward pacifism and are running away from today, while others, especially many in urban ghettoes, have adopted violence as a way of life. They no longer flinch when someone is mugged in the street. They view the gun and knife as survival tools in a society they feel has always "lived by the sword." Television has shown them how to use those tools effectively and provided them with the inspiration to use them. Television has shown them "the promised land" and they will resort to force in order to reach it, if necessary.

In a way, the TV-generation people are a desperate people. They seem to live without much long-range planning, as if sensing impending annihilation. They strive to get as much out of every day as possible, as if there will be no tomorrow. They move through each day as if life were a big "heads and tails" gamble, with the coin flipped, having reached the arc of its flight.

20

An Appeal to Parents

Today's young children are the second TV generation. What they watch on TV and how long they watch will be a major factor in the way they develop as human beings. It will also be a determining factor in the condition of the society in which they have to live, work, and play.

The first TV generation is among us, a bit weird to older people, uneasy and uncertain about itself, dissatisfied with the way previous generations have operated, yearning for change, and bearing behavioral defects which are the result of an overdose of exposure to TV.

Had parents understood television's power to teach what it shows, had they understood its ability to shape attitudes and beliefs, their children's emotional health would be in better shape. Though we can't relive the past, we can reconstruct it to see where we went wrong and make sure those mistakes are never repeated.

The parents of the first TV-generation people, like almost everyone else during the past twenty-five years, never seriously considered what impact television can have on people's behavior, especially children's behavior. Their mistakes were, for the most part, mistakes of omission. After all, how can Mickey Mouse, Popeye, Superman, or the Lone Ranger damage children? How can sitting quietly in front of a TV set hurt a child? Besides, wouldn't the government warn us if television were potentially dangerous?

Most parents throughout the ages have tried to help their children grow into healthy, happy, and useful adults. This natural urge is a tremendous asset. For without it, caring for children would degenerate into a spiritless chore, producing love-starved, emotionally crippled adults.

But, to fulfill his responsibility to his child, a parent needs more than a deep desire to help him. A parent must have knowledge of how to nourish his child's intellectual and emotional growth and how to protect him from forces that could warp his development as a human being.

Television has the potential to hurt children, and parents should know this. But knowing is not enough. Doing something about television is more important. But even that is not enough. The quality of the action parents take is most important. For that, in the end, will have the greatest impact on a child.

Resorting to meaningful action takes effort. Sometimes, lots of it. In taking action, parents must first understand the power of television, not only its capacity to hurt, but also its ability to aid healthy human development. That is a sound principle on which to base a program of home television control. But that principle must be applied wisely. This means knowing what's on TV and being able to distinguish between what will be good and bad for your children. Making these decisions shouldn't be as difficult as it might seem, especially if your children have a relatively short time limit for daily televiewing.

TV Guide should be helpful. However, if very little information is available about a daily show or a weekly series, parents should preview a series to determine whether their children should be allowed to watch it. If there is inadequate information about a TV special, parents shouldn't turn the show on. Such an approach may seem harsh, but allowing a child to see a program which has not been checked out by his parents is like playing Russian Roulette with his psyche.

When parents set up televiewing controls in their home, they should make sure the controls are supervised efficiently and enthusiastically. If parents slip, their kids will most likely drift back to their old TV-watching habits.

Parents must be steadfast in their resolve to control TV viewing at home. But that is not easy, especially in a society that makes so many demands on parents. There is the job, housework, the children's education, Little League baseball practice, music lessons, Girl Scouts, choir practice, club meetings, the bowling league, taxes, shopping, and the soaring cost of living. Not to mention house repairs, installment payments, lodge dues, frustration, self-pity, and an aching back. And on top of all of that, you're expected to control TV watching? "You're crazy!" would be a perfectly natural reaction of the average harassed parent.

But the alternative to TV controls is television freedom. And that is like allowing young children to go on a roller coaster alone or play on a heavily traveled road. There is no alternative, not for parents who love their children.

Parenthood is tough because it is supposed to be a constant creative effort. When a father and mother stop being creative, they become a house security guard and a rooming-house manager and meaningful communication with their children dies. Overwork and excessive worry can kill a parent's creativity.

Establishing TV controls shouldn't be a creativity killer. Before instituting them, parents should reorder their home priorities, consider weeding out some of their pastimes. Of course, it doesn't mean they have to abandon all of their pastimes or hobbies—just the least meaningful ones. After all, people need time for diversion and relaxation, for their spirit needs refreshment. But while parents need periods of relief from work, their children need their love and care. They need guidance on how to cope with the temptations, fads, fashions, and social practices and pressures of the day. They need to be protected from the antisocial modeling on television, a powerful shaper of attitudes, beliefs, and personalities.

Parents who are concerned about TV's impact on their children and are doing something worthwhile about controlling TV viewing in their home need not feel isolated in their struggle. There are organizations which they can tap for inspiration and guidance, organizations like Action for Children's Television, located at 46 Austin Street, Newtonville, Massachusetts.

ACT is an activist group. Besides applying pressure on the federal government, advertisers, and the TV industry to improve the quality of TV programming and advertising, it tries to keep parents abreast of what is good and bad on children's TV through a newsletter produced quarterly. ACT also has materials that parents would find useful in starting and maintaining home TV controls.

Parents should not only educate themselves about TV, they should try, if at all possible, to be active in improving what television offers the public, especially children. This doesn't mean that parents must construct placards and parade in front of their local TV station or a network headquarters or participate in a march on the Federal Communications Commission building in Washington.

A parent can be a television improvement activist by

simply writing a letter to a TV station, network, or advertiser. And the letter doesn't always have to be negative. Often a letter praising a certain program will help to keep the program on the air or inspire TV executives to produce more programs like the one that was praised.

A carbon copy of all letters of complaint should be sent to the FCC and the original letter should make note of where the carbon copy is going.

Viewers' letters have an impact on TV management, especially if they demonstrate sincere concern and are reasonable in tone. An irate letter choked with swear words is quickly tossed in the trash.

TV executives are deeply aware that their companies do not own the right to broadcast. Television station companies actually lease the right to broadcast from the government. This property arrangement gives the people the right to contest a TV company's lease renewal efforts. So letters of legitimate complaint have a way of reminding many television general managers and vice presidents of the possible consequences at lease renewal time.

Parents shouldn't minimize the power of one letter. It would be like underestimating the power of a vote. The letter to a TV station is a democratic way of registering approval or rejection of the performance of the institution of television. Without this kind of check, the commercial television industry would only stress amassing the biggest net profit possible, relegating its public service commitment to one-minute spot announcements that champion innocuous causes.

Whatever reform has taken place in television has come about from pressure outside the industry, much of it springing from grassroots America.

Cigarette advertising was finally chased off TV because of public pressure. Televised violence is being challenged and the industry is beginning to tone down its Saturday morning fare. Vitamin-pill advertisers have been forced to alter their pitch.

Now is not the time for the public to abandon its concern about the quality of TV and its struggle to clean TV up. It is a time when parents must redouble their efforts, helping to work for the day when TV will be safe for their children to watch.

Hopefully, in the future, parents will not have to exercise so much quality control of television; they will be able to allow their children to watch whatever they please within their daily TV-watching time limit without worrying about their kids being exposed to damaging programming and advertising content. But for that to happen, the television industry must stop trying to fool the public.

For too long television corporate executives and their public relations men have regularly reinforced the impression that TV watching is safe no matter what kids watch and no matter how much kids watch. That theme has been drummed into the public with such vigor and frequency that many TV policy makers have learned to believe that myth themselves.

The myth has to be shattered and the TV industry must lead the demolition effort. But more than a propaganda campaign is required. They must do something concrete like creating new children's programming, the kind that would uplift the spirit of the young, arouse their curiosity, sharpen their minds, and expand their vision of the world and its relationship to themselves.

Children's TV program shapers must not only be skilled in television production techniques, they should have an appreciation of TV's power to brainwash and an understanding of what constitutes good and bad TV for children. And they should be willing to work with child psychologists, educators, and researchers in formulating new programs and improving existing ones. They should practice their profession in such a way that their dedication to children supersedes their interest in television. With that kind of an outlook, the child TV viewer will gain from watching children's programs.

The TV industry must no longer allow advertisers to dictate what should or shouldn't be in programs.

If TV executives know in their hearts that TV commercials are bad for kids and their intuition is supported by human-development specialists, then they should have the courage to scrap the TV ad in children's programming and explore new ways to finance television for boys and girls.

Certainly you can't create and maintain TV programs, especially network quality programs, without money, and advertising is commercial television's primary source of revenue. But advertising is not the only source of funding. Government agencies and foundations could be tapped. The TV network and station advertising salesmen would simply have to regear their sales approach. Instead of selling Procter and Gamble and Kellogg's, they would sell institutions like the United States Office of Education or the Ford Foundation. Of course, if the commercial TV networks and local independent stations adopted this funding approach, they would have to turn their children's programming sector into a nonprofit organization. By doing this, the networks and stations would gain considerable public-service credit from the Federal Communications Commission and would build up tremendous good will with the public, while all production, manpower, maintenance, and creative costs would be paid for by the foundation or government. To make up for the loss in net profit revenue, the networks and stations could raise the price of commercials that appear in programs designed for the adult audience.

The federal government should be willing to cooperate in this funding approach because it has been in the
subsidy business for quite a while. If Washington can
subsidize bankrupt railroads and farmers for not growing
crops, it should be able to find funds to support an
effort like children's TV programming, which is concerned with the healthy growth of tender little human
beings who one day will be the citizens and leaders of the
nation. In a small but significant way, the government is
already subsidizing children's TV. It is providing most of
the money to produce *Sesame Street* and *Electric Company*.

When children can watch TV without adult supervi-
sion and not be hurt, television will be on the way to
fulfilling its potential as an instrument that can improve
the quality of life in society. We have had glimpses of the
good it can do. So its potential for good does not have to
be proven.

Television can be used to teach cooperation rather
than exploitation, to teach service to others instead of
selfishness, to teach respect for differences, not disdain
for strangeness. It can teach us to overcome our obsession
for "winning" and fear of "losing." TV can be used to
help draw out man's potential for goodness. For too long
it has played on man's animal nature, glorifying fighting,
quickening his urge for sensuousness, cheapening sex,
separating it from love, and using it to sell cigars and
deodorants. Television can help us to understand man's
unique station on our planet as Earth's highest form of
creation. Through TV we can not only learn to appreciate
different cultures but learn something worthwhile from
them. Television can be used to unite the human family,
for too long a quiet hope and dimming dream of many
people in the past and present.

In the meantime, millions of children, the second TV generation, will continue to turn on TV sets to watch programs and commercials that teach them to be exploiters, sexists, materialists, and racists, that deaden their feelings toward human suffering and champion settling disputes with an uppercut or a gun blast.

NOTES

CHAPTER ONE

1. Dan Anderson, "Determinants of Preschool Children's Attention to Television," Research Proposal submitted to U.S. Department of Health, Education and Welfare, Office of Child Development, July 1972, p. 1.

2. Robert M. Liebert and Rita W. Poulos, "TV for Kiddies, Truth, Goodness, Beauty—and a Little Bit of Brainwash," *Psychology Today*, November 1972, p. 126.

3. Anderson, "Determinants of Preschool Children's Attention to Television," p. 2.

4. Dr. Gerald S. Lesser, "Learning, Teaching, and Television Production for Children: The Experience of Sesame Street," *Harvard Educational Review*, 42 (May 1972): 239.

5. Cristopher Wren, "How to Find the Live Ones on Children's TV," *Saturday Review* (Education), September 16, 1972, p. 61.

6. Charles Silberman, *Crisis in the Classroom*, (New York: Random House, Vintage Books, 1971), p. 32.

7. From an article by William O'Grady, "Preparation of Teachers of Media," *Journal of Aesthetic Education*, 3 (Summer 1969): 9.

8. Marshall McLuhan (Interview with Peebles), *Videocord World*, February 1972, p. 28.

9. Marshall McLuhan, "What TV Is Doing to Your Child," *Family Circle*, March 1967, p. 99.

10. Harry Brecher, *National Enquirer*, November 11, 1973, p. 6.

11. Frank W. Lopez, "How to Watch Television," *Media Ecology Review*, 2, no. 2 (October 9, 1972): 16.

12. *Ibid.*, p. 16.

13. *Ibid.*

14. Philip G. Jones, "The Educational TV in Your Schools May Be Anything but Educational," *American School Board Journal*, March 1974, p. 27.

15. Edward B. Fiske, "Exploring the Mysteries of the Mind," *Spiritual Frontiers* (Evanston, Ill.), 4, no. 3 (Summer 1972): 147.

CHAPTER TWO

1. Dr. John Condry, "Impact of Ads on the Parent-Child Relationship," Boston Association for the Education of Young Children Report, vol. 13, no. 4, April 1972.

2. Reprinted in *Advertising Age*, December 1, 1969, p. 28.

3. Katherine R. Lustman, *"Play,"* (Address delivered at the Third Annual Convention of Action for Children's Television at Yale University, New Haven, Conn., October 16, 1972).

4. *Television Audience*, A. C. Neilsen Co., October 1973, p. 8.

5. Eliot A. Daley, "Is TV Brutalizing Your Child?" *Look*, December 2, 1969, pp. 98-99.

6. Richard L. Tobin, "Murder on Television and the Fourteen-Year-Old," *Saturday Review*, January 8, 1972.

7. *TIO*, Bulletin of the Television Information Office, 1972, under heading "Research and Publications," p. 2.

8. Robert Cirino, *Don't Blame the People* (Los Angeles: Diversity Press, 1972), p. 242.

9. Eli A. Rubinstein, *Report to the Surgeon General, United States Public Health Service, from the Surgeon General's Scientific Advisory Committee on Television and Social Behavior* (Washington, D.C.: Government Printing Office, 1972).

10. "The Media," *Newsweek*, March 6, 1972, p. 55.

11. *Television Audience*, p. 4.

12. Gerald Looney, M.D., M.P.H., "Television and the Child: What Can Be Done?" (Position Paper presented to Section on Child Development, American Academy of Pediatrics, Chicago, Ill., October 17, 1971).

13. *Psychological Abstracts* annually lists all published articles and studies in the field of psychology.

14. Looney, "Television and the Child."

15. *Ibid.*

16. Lee Polk, Informal Remarks at the Third Annual Convention of Action for Children's Television at Yale University, New Haven, Conn., October 16, 1972.

17. Sam S. Baker, *The Permissible Lie* (Boston: Beacon Press, 1971), p. 100.

18. *Special Report: Children and Television, Act Symposium* (Newtonville, Mass.: Action for Children's Television, November 1972), p.1.

19. From an address delivered by Fred Rogers to the Second National Symposium on Children and Television, cosponsored by Action for Children's Television and the American Academy of Pediatrics' Committee on Public Information, Chicago, Ill., October, 1971.

20. Based on a study by psychologists Jack Lyle and Heidi R. Hoffman described in Robert M. Liebert and Rita W. Poulos, "TV for Kiddies: Truth, Goodness, Beauty—and a Little Bit of Brainwash," *Psychology Today*, November 1972, p. 126.

21. Evelyn Sarson, "We As Parents Accuse You of the Five Deadly Sins," *New York Times*, Arts and Leisure Section, Sunday, February 29, 1972, p. 17.

22. Evelyn Sarson, "Schools Make News," *Saturday Review*, August 21, 1971, p. 48.

23. *Ibid.*

24. *Ibid.*

25. "The Media," *Newsweek*, May 31, 1971, p. 71.

CHAPTER FIVE

1. Dr. Edward Palmer, Remarks before International Seminar on Broadcaster/Researcher Cooperation in Mass Communication Research, University of Leicester, Leicester, England, December 19, 1970.

2. Katherine R. Lustman, "Play" (Address delivered at Third Annual Convention of Action for Children's Television at Yale University, New Haven, Conn.) October 16, 1972.

3. Studs Terkel, "Image, Image, on the Tube, Tell Me Who I Am," *Saturday Review*, September 1, 1972, p. 13.

4. W. Penfield, "The Interpretive Cortex," *Science*, 129 (1959): 1719-25.

5. Gerald Looney, M.D., M.P.H., "Television and the Child: What Can Be Done?" (Position Paper presented to Section on Child Development, American Academy of Pediatrics, Chicago, Ill., October 17, 1971), p. 1.

6. Henry J. Skornia, *Television and Society* (New York: McGraw-Hill Book Company, 1965), p. 174.

7. *TV Guide*, February 2, 1974.

8. Jeffrey Schrank, "There Is Only One Mass Medium: A Resource Guide to Commercial Television," *Media and Methods*, February 1974, pp. 32, 33.

9. Norman Mark, *Chicago Daily News*, April 10, 1972.

10. Leonard Berkowitz, "Sex & Violence: We Can't Have It Both Ways," *Psychology Today*, December 1971, p. 23.

11. Vance Packard, *Hidden Persuaders* (New York: Pocket Cardinal Ed., 1958), p. 141.

12. Dr. Gerald S. Lesser, "Learning, Teaching and Television Production for Children: The Experience of Sesame Street," *Harvard Educational Review*, 42, no. 2 (May 1972): 239.

CHAPTER SIX

1. "Arthur Bremer's 'Notes from the Underground,' " *Time*, May 29, 1972, p. 25.
2. Max Lerner, "Colleges and the Urban Crisis," in Fred F. Harderoad, ed., *Issues of the Seventies* (San Francisco: Jossey-Bass, 1970), pp. 33, 34.

CHAPTER SEVEN

1. "Living with Crime, U.S.A.," *Newsweek*, December 18, 1972, p. 33.
2. *Profiles of Children: White House Conference on Children*, (Washington, D.C.: Government Printing Office, 1970), p. 78.
3. "Crime in America," *National Enquirer*, April 15, 1973, p. 21.
4. Jerry Rubin, *Do It!* (New York: Ballantine Books, 1970).
5. Richard L. Tobin, "Murder on Television and the Fourteen-Year-Old," *Saturday Review*, January 8, 1972, p. 39.
6. Evelyn Kaye Sarson, "How TV Threatens Your Child," *Parents' Magazine*, August 1972, p. 92.
7. Tobin, "Murder on Television and the Fourteen-Year-Old," p. 39.
8. Phillip Nobile, "TV Violence Question Settled," *Springfield Republican*, April 9, 1972.
9. *Television and Children: A Threat or a Promise*, Booklet of the Publications Division of the National Education Association, Hyattsville, Md. (unnumbered pages).

10. "The Media," *Newsweek,* March 6, 1972, p. 56.

11. *Ibid.*

12. Sarson, "How TV Threatens Your Child," p. 92.

13. Robert M. Liebert and Rita W. Poulos, "TV for Kiddies, Truth, Goodness, Beauty—and a Little Bit of Brainwash," *Psychology Today,* November 1972, p. 123.

14. "Violence on Children's TV Is Hazardous to Health," *ACT,* 3, no. 1 (Spring/Summer 1972): 2.

15. *Ibid.*

16. Liebert and Poulos, "TV for Kiddies," p. 128.

17. "The Media," *Newsweek,* March 6, 1972, p. 55.

18. *Ibid.*

19. Dorothy Rogers, *Issues in Child Psychology* (Belmont, Calif.: Brooks/Cole, 1969).

20. George Green, "My Turn," *Newsweek,* February 26, 1973, p. 9.

21. Haim Ginott, "How to Drive Your Child Sane," *Life,* October 20, 1972, p. 54.

22. Dr. Richard H. Granger, "Childhood Professionals Look at Children's Television" (Paper presented at the Third Annual Convention of Action for Children's Television at Yale University, New Haven, Conn., October 16, 1972).

CHAPTER EIGHT

1. Robert Cirino, *Don't Blame the People* (Los Angeles: Diversity Press, 1972), p. 148.

2. From *Changing Times,* July 1968.

3. Arnold Barban, "The Dilemma of Integrated Advertising," *Journal of Business,* October 1969, p. 479.

4. *Special Report: Children and Television, ACT Symposium* (Newtonville, Mass.: Action for Children's Television, November 1972), p. 3.

CHAPTER NINE

1. Sarah Sternglands and Lisa Serbin, "A Study: An Analysis of the Sex Roles Presented on Children's TV Programs" (Presented at a Meeting of Society for Research in Child Development, Philadelphia, March 1973).

CHAPTER TEN

1. Ven H. Bagdikian, *The Information Machines, Their Impact on Men and the Media* (New York: Harper & Row, 1971), p. 289.

CHAPTER ELEVEN

1. Richard L. Tobin, "Murder on Television and the Fourteen-Year-Old," *Saturday Review*, January 8, 1972, p. 39.

CHAPTER TWELVE

1. *The Network Project: Control of Information*, Bulletin of Columbia University, New York, N.Y., no. 3, March 1973, p. 3; Albert C. Book and Norman D. Cary, *The Television Commercial: Creativity and Craftsmanship* (New York: Decker Communications, 1970), p. 2.
2. Television Bureau of Advertising, New York, March 13 communication with author.
3. Erik Barnouw, *The Image Empire* (New York: Oxford University Press, 1972), p. 6.
4. "As We See It," *TV Guide*, December 6-22, 1972, p.2.

5. Eliot Aronson, *The Social Animal* (New York: Viking, 1972).

6. Vance Packard, *Hidden Persuaders* (New York: Pocket Cardinal Ed., 1958), p. 25.

7. Book and Cary, *The Television Commercial*, p. 3.

8. William D. Wells, "Communicating with Children," *Journal of Advertising Research*, February 14, 1965.

9. Dr. Joseph T. Plummer, "A Theoretical View of Advertising Communication, *"Journal of Communication*, 21, no. 4 (December 1971): 318.

10. *Ibid.*, p. 319.

11. *Ibid.*

12. Vance Packard, *Hidden Persuaders* (New York: Pocket Cardinal Ed., 1958), p. 137.

13. *Ibid.*

14. Herbert Kuptenberg, "Your Kids Need Better TV—You Can Help," *Parade*, January 30, 1972.

15. "The TV Generation," *Changing Times*, July 1968, p. 46.

16. Peggy Charren, "The Child Market," Boston Association for the Education of Young Children Report, vol. 13, no. 4, April 1972. (She took quote from *Broadcasting*, June 30, 1969.)

17. Joan Ganz Cooney, "Isn't It Time We Put the Children First?" *New York Times*, Arts and Leisure Section, Sunday, December 3, 1972, p. 17.

18. Sam Sinclair Baker, *The Permissible Lie* (Boston: Beacon Press, 1971), p. 5.

19. *Ibid.*

20. Dr. F. Earle Barcus, *Saturday Children's Television: A Report of TV Programming and Advertising on Boston Commercial Television* (Newtonville, Mass.: Action for Children's Television, July 1971), pp. 45, 46.

21. *Ibid.*

22. Vance Packard, *Hidden Persuaders* (New York: Pocket Cardinal Ed., 1958), p. 136.

23. Satu Repo, *This Book Is about Schools* (New York: Random House, Vintage Books, 1970), p. 52.

CHAPTER THIRTEEN

1. Dr. Urie Bronfenbrenner, (Speech delivered at the ABC-TV Children's Television Workshop, New York City, 1971).

2. Richard Held and Alan Hein, "Movement Produced Stimulation in the Development of Visually Guided Behavior," *Journal of Comparative and Physiological Psychology,* 56 (1963): 872-76.

3. Dr. Katherine R. Lustman, "Play" (Address delivered at the Third Annual Convention of Action for Children's Television, Yale University, New Haven, Conn., October 17, 1972).

4. Jack Lyle and Heidi R. Hoffman, "Children's Use of Television and Other Media," In E. Rubenstein, G. Comstock, and J. Murray, eds., *Television and Social Behavior,* 4 (Washington, D.C.: Government Printing Office, 1972): 180.

CHAPTER FOURTEEN

1. Dr. Urie Bronfenbrenner, Speech delivered to the ABC-TV Children's Television Workshop, New York City, 1971.

2. Alan Markfield, "Four Leading Experts on Marriage Blame Television for Soaring Divorce Rate," *National Enquirer,* April 3, 1973.

3. *Ibid.*

CHAPTER FIFTEEN

1. James G. Cunningham, "Epilepsy Causes and Control," *Progress*, Gaines Dog Research Bulletin (White Plains, N.Y., Spring 1972) p. 3.
2. Dr. John Ott, "Responses of Psychological and Physiological Functions to Environmental Radiation Stress," *Journal of Learning Disabilities*, 1, no. 6 (June 1968): 351, 352.
3. *Ibid.*, p. 352.
4. *Ibid.*, pp. 353, 354.
5. "Those Tired Children," *Time*, November 6, 1964.
6. Robert Cirino, *Don't Blame the People* (Los Angeles: Diversity Press, 1971), p. 99.
7. Ott, "Responses of Psychological and Physiological Functions to Environmental Radiation Stress," p. 352.
8. "To View or Not to View?" pamphlet issued by American Optometric Association, St. Louis, Mo., n.d., unnumbered pages.
9. Frank W. Lopez, "How to Watch Television," *Media Ecology Review*, 2, no. 2 (October 9, 1972): 15.
10. Marshall McLuhan, "What TV Is Doing to Your Children," *Family Circle*, March 1967, p. 100.
11. "To View or Not to View?"
12. Lopez, "How to Watch Television," p. 4.
13. *Ibid., p. 15.*

CHAPTER SEVENTEEN

1. Gerald Looney, M.D., M.P.H., "Television and the Child: What Can Be Done?" (Position Paper presented to Section on Child Development, American Academy of Pediatrics, Chicago, Ill., October 17, 1971).
2. *Ibid.*

3. Robert Louis Shayon, TV-Radio Column, *Saturday Review*, May 9, 1970.

4. *Newsweek*, May 22, 1972, p. 99A.

5. Robert E. Sutton, "Television's Children," *Learning*, September 1973.

CHAPTER EIGHTEEN

1. "Child Development and the Mass Media," *Report to the President, White House Conference on Children* (Washington, D.C.: Government Printing Office, July 1970), p. 326.

2. "The TV Generation," *Changing Times*, July 1968, p. 47.

3. Haim G. Ginott, *Between Parent and Child* (New York: Macmillan Co., Avon, 1965), pp. 119, 120.

CHAPTER NINETEEN

1. Jerry Rubin, *Do It!* (New York: Ballantine Books, 1970), pp. 107-8.